STILL STEAMING

The Guide to
Britain's Steam Railways
1998/99

EDITOR
Mike Ross

Second Edition

British Library Cataloguing in Publication Data
A catalogue record for this book is available from the British Library

ISBN 1-86223-018-8

Printed by Adlard Print & Typesetting Services, The Old School, The Green, Ruddington, Notts. NG11 6HH

FOREWORD

Following the successful launch of Still Steaming in 1997 we have enlarged this 2nd edition to include no less than 10 new locations!

We were greatly impressed by the friendly and cooperative manner of the staff and helpers of the railways which we selected to appear in this book, and wish to thank them all for the help they have given.

Although we believe that the information contained in this guide is accurate at the time of going to press, we, and the Railways and Museums itemised, are unable to accept liability for any loss, damage, distress or injury suffered as a result of any inaccuracies included. Furthermore, we and the Railways are unable to guarantee operating and opening times which may always be subject to cancellation without notice.

If you feel we should include other locations or information in future editions, please let us know so that we may give them consideration.

We would like to thank you for buying this guide and wish you 'Happy Steaming'.

Mike Ross
EDITOR

Note: Further copies of this guide may be obtained, post free, from our address on the opposite page.

CONTENTS

ACKNOWLEDGMENTS

We regret that we have been unable to include captions for the photographs which are included in this publication due to lack of space.

Many were taken by our own photographer but we do thank the railways which so generously provided the remaining photographs.

We aim to improve the quality of photographs in future editions and welcome any which readers may wish to supply.

NATIONAL RAILWAY MUSEUM

Address: National Railway Museum, Leeman Road, York YO2 4XJ **Telephone Nº:** (01904) 621261 **Year Formed:** 1975 **Location of Line:** York **Length of Line:** Short demonstration line	**Nº of Steam Locos:** 78 **Nº of Other Locos:** 36 **Nº of Members:** 3,000 **Annual Membership Fee:** £18.00 **Approx Nº of Visitors P.A.:** 400,000

GENERAL INFORMATION

Nearest Railtrack Station: York (¼ mile)
Nearest Bus Station: York (¼ mile)
Car Parking: On site long stay car park
Coach Parking: On site – free to pre-booked groups
Souvenir Shop(s): Yes
Food & Drinks: Yes

SPECIAL INFORMATION

The Museum is the largest of its kind in the world, housing the Nation's collection of locomotives, carriages, uniforms, posters and an extensive photographic archive. Special events and exhibitions run throughout the year. The Museum is the home of the Mallard – the fastest steam locomotive in the world.

OPERATING INFORMATION

Opening Times: Open daily 10.00am to 6.00pm (closed on 24th, 25th and 26th of December)
Steam Working: School holidays
Prices: Adult (ages 17+) £4.95
Child (ages 4-16) £3.15
O.A.P. £3.95
Family £14.50
(2 adults + 3 children)
Concessions £3.60

Detailed Directions by Car:
The Museum is located in the centre of York, just behind the Railway Station. It is clearly signposted from all approaches to York.

NATIONAL
RAILWAY
MUSEUM

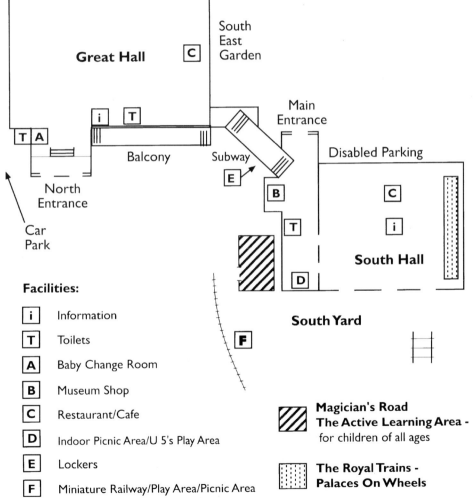

Great Hall

South
East
Garden

[C]

Main
Entrance

[i] [T]

[T] [A]

Balcony

Subway

[E]

Disabled Parking

North
Entrance

[B]

[T]

[C]

[i]

Car
Park

South Hall

[D]

Facilities:

[i] Information

[T] Toilets

[A] Baby Change Room

[B] Museum Shop

[C] Restaurant/Cafe

[D] Indoor Picnic Area/U 5's Play Area

[E] Lockers

[F] Miniature Railway/Play Area/Picnic Area

South Yard

[F]

Magician's Road
The Active Learning Area -
for children of all ages

The Royal Trains -
Palaces On Wheels

AVON VALLEY RAILWAY

Address: Bitton Station, Bath Road, Willsbridge, Bristol BS30 6ED	**Nº of Steam Locos:** 6
Telephone Nº: (0117) 932-7296	**Nº of Other Locos:** 3
Year Formed: 1973	**Nº of Members:** Approximately 500
Location of Line: Midway between Bristol and Bath on A431	**Annual Membership Fee:** £10.00
Length of Line: 2 miles	**Approx Nº of Visitors P.A.:** 70,000

GENERAL INFORMATION

Nearest Railtrack Station: Keynsham (1½ miles)
Nearest Bus Station: Bristol or Bath (7 miles)
Car Parking: Available at Bitton Station
Coach Parking: Available at Bitton Station
Souvenir Shop(s): Yes
Food & Drinks: Yes

SPECIAL INFORMATION

The line is currently being extended through the scenic Avon Valley towards Bath.

OPERATING INFORMATION

Opening Times: Every Sunday May to September inclusive. Also Bank Holiday Mondays and Christmas. Open from 10.30am to 6.00pm
Steam Working: 11.00am to 5.00pm
Prices: Adult £3.00
Child £1.50
Family Tickets £8.50

Detailed Directions by Car:
From All Parts: Exit the M4 at Junction 18. Follow the A46 towards Bath and at the junction with the A420 turn right towards Bristol. At Bridge Yate turn left onto the A4175 and continue until you reach the A431. Turn right and Bitton Station is 100 yards on the right.

BALA LAKE RAILWAY

Address: Bala Lake Railway,
Llanuwchllyn, Gwynedd, LL23 7DD
Telephone Nº: (01678) 540666
Year Formed: 1972
Location of Line: Llanuwchllyn to Bala
Length of Line: 4½ miles

Nº of Steam Locos: 3
Nº of Other Locos: –
Nº of Members: –
Annual Membership Fee: –
Approx Nº of Visitors P.A.: 20,000
Gauge: 1 foot 11 five-eighth inches

GENERAL INFORMATION

Nearest Railtrack Station: Wrexham (40 miles)
Nearest Bus Station: Wrexham (40 miles)
Car Parking: Adequate parking in Llanuwchllyn
Coach Parking: At Llanuwchllyn or in Bala Town Centre
Souvenir Shop(s): Yes
Food & Drinks: Yes – unlicensed!

SPECIAL INFORMATION

Bala Lake Railway is a narrow-gauge railway which follows 4½ miles of the former Ruabon to Barmouth G.W.R. line.

OPERATING INFORMATION

Opening Times: 10th April to 4th October
Steam Working: All advertised services are steam hauled
Prices: Adult Return £6.00
Child Return £1.00 (when with an Adult)
Family Return – From £7.00

Detailed Directions by Car:
From All Parts: The railway is situated off the A494 Bala to Dolgellau road which is accessible from the national motorways via the A5 or A55.

THE BATTLEFIELD LINE

Address: The Battlefield Line, Shackerstone Station, Shackerstone, Warwickshire CV13 6NW	**N° of Steam Locos:** 7
Telephone N°: (01827) 880754	**N° of Other Locos:** 8
Year Formed: 1968	**N° of Members:** 500 approximately
Location of Line: North West of Market Bosworth	**Annual Membership Fee:** £11.00 Adult; £17.50 Family
Length of Line: 5 miles	**Approx N° of Visitors P.A.:** 50,000
	Gauge: Standard

GENERAL INFORMATION

Nearest Railtrack Station: Nuneaton (9 miles)
Nearest Bus Station: Nuneaton & Hinckley (9 miles)
Car Parking: Ample free parking available
Coach Parking: Can cater for coach parties
Souvenir Shop(s): Yes
Food & Drinks: Yes – Station Buffet

SPECIAL INFORMATION

Adjoining the Ashby Canal set in South Leicester-shire's beautiful countryside, the Southern Terminus Station, Shenton, sits at the foot of the Battle of Bosworth Site (1485).

OPERATING INFORMATION

Operating Info: 2nd week in March to the last week in November. Please phone for further details
Opening Times: 10.30am to 6.00pm
Steam Working: 11.15am, 12.30pm, 1.45pm & 4.15pm on Saturdays & Sundays
Prices: Adult Return £5.00
Child Return £2.50
O.A.P. Return £2.50

Detailed Directions by Car:
Follow the brown tourist signs from the A444 or A447 heading towards the market town of Market Bosworth. Continue towards the villages of Congerstone & Shackerstone and finally to Shackerstone Station. Access is only available via the Old Trackbed.

BEAMISH OPEN AIR MUSEUM

Address: Beamish North of England Open Air Museum, Co. Durham DH9 0RG **Telephone N°**: (01207) 231811 **Year Formed**: 1970 **Location of Line**: None **Length of Line**: –	**N° of Steam Locos**: 8 **N° of Other Locos**: 3 **N° of Members**: – **Annual Membership Fee**: – **Approx N° of Visitors P.A.**: 365,000

GENERAL INFORMATION

Nearest Railtrack Station: Newcastle Central (8 miles); Durham City (12 miles)
Nearest Bus Station: Durham (12 miles), Newcastle (8 miles)
Car Parking: Free parking for 2,000 cars
Coach Parking: Free parking for 40 coaches
Souvenir Shop(s): Yes
Food & Drinks: Yes – self service tea room & licensed period pub. Coffee shop in Summer.

SPECIAL INFORMATION

Beamish recreates Northern life in the early 1800's and 1900's in the Town, Colliery Village, Home Farm, Pockerley Manor and Railway Station, complete with goods yard, signal box, locomotives and rolling stock.

OPERATING INFORMATION

Opening Times: Open all year round from 10.00am to 4.00pm in the Winter – 5.00 or 6.00pm in the Summer. Closed Mondays and Fridays in the Winter.
N.B. There is a reduced operation in the Winter.
Steam Working: –
Prices: Adult £8.00 in Summer; £3.00 in Winter
 Child £5.00 in Summer; £2.00 in Winter
 O.A.P. £6.00 in Summer; £3.00 in Winter
 Children under 5 are admitted free

Detailed Directions by Car:
From North & South: Follow the A1(M) to Junction 63 (Chester-le-street) and then take A693 for 4 miles to-wards Stanley; From North-West: Take the A68 south to Castleside near Consett and follow the signs on the A692 and A693 via Stanley.

BIRMINGHAM RAILWAY MUSEUM

Address: 670 Warwick Road, Tyseley, Birmingham	**N⁰ of Steam Locos:** 19 (12 undergoing restoration)
Telephone N⁰: (0121) 707-4696	**N⁰ of Other Locos:** 13
Year Formed: 1969	**N⁰ of Members:** –
Location of Museum: Tyseley	**Approx N⁰ of Visitors P.A.:** 15,000
Length of Line: A third of a mile	**Gauge:** Standard

GENERAL INFORMATION

Nearest Railtrack Station: Tyseley (5 mins. walk)
Nearest Bus Station: Birmingham. Bus Stop at Reddings Lane – 2 minutes walk (Bus route 37 passes the entrance)
Car Parking: 200 spaces at Railway site
Coach Parking: Space at Railway site
Souvenir Shop(s): Yes
Food & Drinks: Yes – weekends & holidays only

SPECIAL INFORMATION

The Museum runs a large workshop which produces refurbished locomotives. Driver training courses are available at weekends – bookings for these courses are essential.

OPERATING INFORMATION

Opening Times: From the first Sunday in April to October. 10.00am to 5.00pm in the Summer; 10.00am to 4.00pm in the Winter. Driver training courses are available most weekends.
Steam Working: Weekends and School holidays only
Prices: Adult Return £2.50
Child Return £1.25
Family Return £6.25

Detailed Directions by Car:
From the North: Exit the M6 at Junction 6 and take A41 ring road towards Solihull; From the South: Exit the M42 at Junction 5 and take the A41 towards Birmingham.

THE BLUEBELL RAILWAY

Address: The Bluebell Railway, Sheffield Park Station, Nr. Uckfield, East Sussex, TN22 3QL
Telephone Nº: (0182) 572-3777
Information Line: (0182) 572-2370
Year Formed: 1959
Location of Line: Nr. Uckfield, E. Sussex
Length of Line: 9 miles

Nº of Steam Locos: Over 30 with up to 3 in operation on any given day
Nº of Other Locos: –
Nº of Members: 8,000
Annual Membership Fee: £12.00 Adult
Approx Nº of Visitors P.A.: 150,000
Gauge: Standard

GENERAL INFORMATION

Nearest Railtrack Station: East Grinstead (2 miles) with a bus connection
Nearest Bus Station: East Grinstead
Car Parking: Parking at Sheffield Park and Horsted Keynes Stations.
Coach Parking: Sheffield Park is best
Souvenir Shop(s): Yes
Food & Drinks: Yes – buffets and licensed bars & restaurant

SPECIAL INFORMATION

The Railway runs 'Wine and Dine' trains on Saturday evenings and Sunday lunchtimes. There is also a museum and model railway at Sheffield Park Station.

OPERATING INFORMATION

Opening Times: Every weekend and also daily from May to September inclusive. Also open during School holidays and Santa Specials over Christmas Holidays. Approximately 10.00am to 6.00pm
Steam Working: As above
Prices: Adult Return £7.40
Child Return £3.70
Family Return £19.90
(2 adults + up to 3 children)

Detailed Directions by Car:
Sheffield Park Station is situated on the A275 Wych Cross to Lewes road. Horsted Keynes Station is signposted from the B2028 Lingfield to Haywards Heath road.

BODMIN & WENFORD RAILWAY

Address: Bodmin General Station, Losthwithiel Road, Bodmin, Cornwall PL31 1AQ	**Length of Line:** 6½ miles
	N° of Steam Locos: 10
	N° of Other Locos: 9
Telephone N°: (01208) 73666	**N° of Members:** 850
Year Formed: 1984	**Annual Membership Fee:** £8.00
Location of Line: Bodmin Parkway Station to Bodmin General and Boscarne.	**Approx N° of Visitors P.A.:** 40,000+
	Gauge: Standard

GENERAL INFORMATION

Nearest Railtrack Station: Bodmin Parkway
Nearest Bus Station: Bodmin (½ mile)
Car Parking: Free parking at site
Coach Parking: Free parking at site
Souvenir Shop(s): Yes
Food & Drinks: Yes

SPECIAL INFORMATION

The Railway has steep gradients and there are two different branches to choose from Bodmin General.

OPERATING INFORMATION

Opening Times: Daily from June to the end of September. Wednesdays & Sundays April, May & October. Weekends in December. Various other dates also.
Steam Working: Usually trains are steam-hauled except for most Saturdays when Diesels are used.
Prices: Adult Return £7.50
Child Return £4.00
Family Return £20.00
(2 adults + up to 4 children)
N.B. Through tickets to "Bodmin & Wenford Railway" are available from all Railtrack stations.

Detailed Directions by Car:
From the A30/A38 follow the signs to Bodmin Town Centre then follow the brown tourist signs to the Steam Railway on the B3268 Losthwithiel Road.

BO'NESS & KINNEIL RAILWAY

Address: Bo'ness Station, Union Street, Bo'ness, West Lothian   EH51 9AQ
Telephone Nº: (01506) 822298
Year Formed: 1981
Location of Line: Bo'ness to Birkhill
Length of Line: 3½ miles

Nº of Steam Locos: 21
Nº of Other Locos: 18
Nº of Members: 1,300
Annual Membership Fee: £11.00
Approx Nº of Visitors P.A.: 45,000
Gauge: Standard

GENERAL INFORMATION

Nearest Railtrack Station: Linlithgow (3 miles)
Nearest Bus Station: Bo'ness (½ mile)
Car Parking: Free parking at Bo'ness and Birkhill Stations
Coach Parking: Free parking at Bo'ness Station
Souvenir Shop(s): Yes
Food & Drinks: Yes

SPECIAL INFORMATION

The Scottish Railway Exhibition is situated at Bo'ness and conducted tours are also available of the caverns of Birkhill Mine.

OPERATING INFORMATION

Opening Times: Weekends from April to mid October. Also Tuesday to Sunday from July to the end of August.
Steam Working: The first train leaves at 11.20am and the last at 4.30pm
Prices: Adult Return £3.90
             Child Return £1.90
             Family Return £9.70

Detailed Directions by Car:
From Edinburgh: Take the M9 and exit at Junction 3. Then take the A904 to Bo'ness; From Glasgow: Take the M80 to M876 and then M9 (South). Exit at Junction 5 and take A904 to Bo'ness; From the North: Take M9 (South), exit at Junction 5, then take A904 to Bo'ness; From Fife: Leave the A90 after the Forth Bridge, then take A904 to Bo'ness.

BOWES RAILWAY

Address: Bowes Railway, Springwell Village, Gateshead, Tyne & Wear NE9 7QJ
Telephone Nº: (0191) 416-1847
Year Formed: 1976
Location of Line: –
Length of Line: Springwell Village

Nº of Steam Locos: 3 (only 1 operating)
Nº of Other Locos: 4
Nº of Members: Approximately 70
Annual Membership Fee: £10.00
Approx Nº of Visitors P.A.: 3,000
Gauge: Standard

GENERAL INFORMATION

Nearest Railtrack Station: Newcastle Central (3 miles)
Nearest Bus Station: Gateshead Interchange (2 miles)
Car Parking: Free parking at site
Coach Parking: Free parking at site
Souvenir Shop(s): Yes
Food & Drinks: Yes

SPECIAL INFORMATION

Designed by George Stephenson and opened in 1826, the Railway is a scheduled Ancient Monument operating unique preserved standard gauge rope-hauled inclines as well as steam hauled passenger trains.

OPERATING INFORMATION

Opening Times: (1998 dates) 24th & 25th May, 28th June, 6th July, 30th & 31st August and 27th September. Open 11.00am to 5.00pm on operating days.
Steam Working: Every 30 minutes
Prices: Adult Return £1.00
Child Return 50p
Senior Citizens 50p
(Prices include train ride + Rope Haulage demonstration)

Detailed Directions by Car:
From A1 (Northbound): Follow the A194(M) to the Tyne Tunnel and turn left at the sign for Springwell; From A1 (Southbound): Take the turn off left for the B1288 to Springwell and Wrekenton.

BRECON MOUNTAIN RAILWAY

Address: Pant Station, Dowlais, Merthyr Tydfil   CF48 2UP
Telephone Nº: (01685) 722988
Year Formed: 1980
Location of Line: North of Merthyr Tydfil – 1 mile from the A465
Gauge: 1 foot 11¾ inches

Length of Line: 3½ miles
Nº of Steam Locos: 7
Nº of Other Locos: 2
Nº of Members: –
Annual Membership Fee: –
Approx Nº of Visitors P.A.: 66,000

GENERAL INFORMATION

Nearest Railtrack Station: Merthyr Tydfil (3 miles)
Nearest Bus Station: Merthyr Tydfil (3 miles)
Car Parking: Available at Pant Station
Coach Parking: Available at Pant Station
Souvenir Shop(s): Yes
Food & Drinks: Yes – including licensed restaurant

SPECIAL INFORMATION

It is possible to take a break before the return journey at Pontsticill to have a picnic, take a forest walk or visit the lakeside snackbar.

OPERATING INFORMATION

Opening Times: Weekends from end of March to end of September. Tuesdays, Wednesdays, Thursdays & Sundays in October. Daily from 23rd May to 13th September. Open during Easter Holidays. Closed some Mondays & Fridays in May and September.
Steam Working: Generally from 10.45am to 3.45pm when open, although sometimes opens at 12.00pm or closes at 5.00pm.
Prices: Adult Return £5.90
Child Return (15 and under) £2.95
Dogs or Bicycles 95p
Family Rate – The first two children can travel for £1.60 when accompanied by an adult.

Detailed Directions by Car:
Exit the M4 at Junction 32 and take the A470 to Merthyr Tydfil. Go onto the A465 and follow the brown tourist signs for the railway.

BRESSINGHAM STEAM MUSEUM

Address: Bressingham Steam Museum, Bressingham, Diss, Norfolk IP22 2AB	**Nº of Steam Locos:** Many Steam locos
Telephone Nº: (01379) 687386	**Nº of Other Locos:** –
Year Formed: Mid 50's	**Nº of Members:** 70 volunteers
Location of Line: Bressingham, Near Diss	**Annual Membership Fee:** –
Length of Line: 5 miles in total (3 lines)	**Approx Nº of Visitors P.A.:** 95,000+
	Gauge: Standard & 3 Narrow gauge lines

GENERAL INFORMATION

Nearest Railtrack Station: Diss (2½ miles)
Nearest Bus Station: Bressingham (1¼ miles)
Car Parking: Free parking for 400 cars available
Coach Parking: Free parking for 30 coaches
Souvenir Shop(s): Yes
Food & Drinks: Yes

SPECIAL INFORMATION

In addition to Steam locomotives, Bressingham has a large selection of steam traction engines and fixed steam engines together with a Fire Engine Museum. Bressingham also has extensive gardens and a large plant nursery.

OPERATING INFORMATION

Opening Times: Daily from Easter to 2nd November 10.30am to 5.00pm
Steam Working: All days, but 'Full Steam' days on Thursdays and Sundays have more trains and steam demonstrations running.
Prices: Adult £2.50 to £5.00
    Child £1.50 to £3.00
    Family £12.00 to £23.00

Detailed Directions by Car:
From All Parts: Take the A11 to Thetford and then follow the A1066 towards Diss for Bressingham. The Museum is signposted by the brown tourist signs.

BRISTOL HARBOUR RAILWAY

Address: Bristol Industrial Museum, Princes Wharf, City Docks, Bristol, BS1 4RN
Telephone N°: (0117) 925-1470
Year Formed: 1978
Location of Line: South side of the Floating Harbour

Length of Line: ½ mile
N° of Steam Locos: 2
N° of Other Locos: 1
N° of Members: –
Annual Membership Fee: –
Approx N° of Visitors P.A.: 70,000

GENERAL INFORMATION

Nearest Railtrack Station: Bristol Temple Meads (1 mile)
Nearest Bus Station: City Centre (½ mile)
Car Parking: Parking available at site
Coach Parking: Drop off and Pick up only
Souvenir Shop(s): Yes
Food & Drinks: No

SPECIAL INFORMATION

The Railway is one of the attractions of the Bristol Industrial Museum which has over 400 exhibits to see, housed in historic transit sheds by a dockside location.

OPERATING INFORMATION

Opening Times: Saturday to Wednesday from April to October. Weekends only from November to March. Open 10.00am to 5.00pm
Steam Working: When the Museum is open.
Prices: Adult £1.00
Child 50p
N.B. Admission is Free of Charge on Sundays.

Detailed Directions by Car:
From All Parts: Follow signs to Bristol City Centre and then the Brown Tourist signs for the Museum. A good landmark to look out for are the 4 huge quayside cranes.

BUCKINGHAMSHIRE RAILWAY CENTRE

Address: Quainton Road Station, Quainton, Aylesbury, Bucks.   HP22 4BY
Telephone Nº: (01296) 655720
Year Formed: 1969
Location of Line: At Quainton on the old Metropolitan/Great Central Line
Length of Line: 2 × ½ mile demo tracks

Nº of Steam Locos: 35
Nº of Other Locos: 6
Nº of Members: 1,000
Annual Membership Fee: £12.00
Approx Nº of Visitors P.A.: 35,000
Gauge: Standard

GENERAL INFORMATION

Nearest Railtrack Station: Aylesbury (6 miles)
Nearest Bus Station: Aylesbury
Car Parking: Free parking for 500 cars available
Coach Parking: Free parking for 30 coaches
Souvenir Shop(s): Yes
Food & Drinks: Yes

SPECIAL INFORMATION

In addition to a large collection of locomotives and carriages, the Centre has an extensive outdoor miniature railway system.

OPERATING INFO

Opening Times: Sundays and Bank Holidays from Easter to 30th October. Also Wednesdays in July and August. Open most Weekends April to October and also some in December. Open from 11.00am to 4.00pm and sometimes until 6.00pm
Steam Working: As above
Prices: Adult £4.50
Child £3.00
Family £14.00
(2 adults + up to 4 children)

Detailed Directions by Car:
The Buckinghamshire Railway Centre is signposted off the A41 Aylesbury to Bicester Road at Waddesdon and off the A413 Buckingham to Aylesbury road at Whitchurch. Junctions 7, 8 and 9 of the M40 are all close by.

BURE VALLEY RAILWAY

Address: Aylsham Station, Norwich Road, Aylsham, Norfolk   NR11 6BW
Telephone Nº: (01263) 733858
Year Formed: 1989
Location of Line: Between Aylsham & Wroxham
Length of Line: 9 miles

Nº of Steam Locos: 4
Nº of Other Locos: 3
Nº of Members: Approximately 300
Annual Membership Fee: £12.50
Approx Nº of Visitors P.A.: 80,000
Gauge: 15 inches

GENERAL INFORMATION

Nearest Railtrack Station: Wroxham (adjacent)
Nearest Bus Station: Aylsham (bus passes station)
Car Parking: Free parking at Aylsham & Wroxham Stations
Coach Parking: As above
Souvenir Shop(s): Yes at both Stations
Food & Drinks: Yes at both Stations

SPECIAL INFORMATION

Boat trains connect at Wroxham with 1½ hour cruise on the Norfolk Broads. Steam Locomotive driving courses are available in off-peak periods.

OPERATING INFORMATION

Opening Times: Various dates from 4th April to the end of October. Daily from June to August. Closed Fridays & Saturdays in June. Trains run from 10.15am to 5.15pm on most days when open.
Steam Working: Most trains are steam hauled
Prices: Adult Return £6.90
              Child Return £3.60
              Family Return £19.00
                     (2 adults + 2 children)
Single fares and intermediate station fares are also available.

Detailed Directions by Car:
From Norwich: Aylsham Station is midway between Norwich and Cromer on the A140 – follow the Aylsham Town Centre signs. Wroxham Station is adjacent to the Wroxham British Rail Station – take the A1151 from Norwich; From King's Lynn: Take A148 and B1354 to reach Aylsham Station.

CADEBY LIGHT RAILWAY

Address: The Old Rectory, Cadeby, Nuneaton, Warks. CV13 0AS	**Nº of Steam Locos:** 3
Telephone Nº: (01455) 290462	**Nº of Other Locos:** 15
Year Formed: 1961	**Nº of Members:** −
Location of Line: 1 mile from Market Bosworth, 6 miles from Hinckley	**Annual Membership Fee:** −
Length of Line: 75 yards	**Approx Nº of Visitors P.A.:** −
	Gauge: 2 feet

GENERAL INFORMATION

Nearest Railtrack Station: Hinckley (6 miles)
Nearest Bus Station: Market Bosworth (1 mile)
Car Parking: Free parking at site
Coach Parking: Roadside parking
Souvenir Shop(s): Yes
Food & Drinks: Yes

SPECIAL INFORMATION

A new museum was opened in 1990, 'The Boston Collection', encompassing the lifetime collection of the late Reverend Teddy Boston and his family. The narrow gauge railway running in the grounds of the old rectory has been saved by Teddy Boston's widow and a small band of dedicated supporters.

OPERATING INFORMATION

Opening Times: 2nd Saturday of every month plus specials – please phone for details.
Steam Working: As above.
Prices: Free, but donations are requested.

Detailed Directions by Car:
Exit the M1 at Junction 18 and take the A5 to Hinckley. From Hinckley take the A447 to Cadeby.

CALEDONIAN RAILWAY

Address: The Station, 2 Park Road, Brechin, Angus DD9 7AF
Telephone Nº: (01674) 810318
Year Formed: 1979
Location of Line: From Brechin to Bridge of Dun
Length of Line: 4 miles

Nº of Steam Locos: 7
Nº of Other Locos: 8
Nº of Members: 250
Annual Membership Fee: Adult £10.00; Family £15.00; OAP/Junior £5.00
Approx Nº of Visitors P.A.: 10,000
Gauge: Standard

GENERAL INFORMATION

Nearest Railtrack Station: Montrose (4½ miles)
Nearest Bus Station: Brechin (200 yards)
Car Parking: Ample free parking at both Stations
Coach Parking: Free parking at both Stations
Souvenir Shop(s): Yes
Food & Drinks: Yes – Restaurant on Platform 2 at Brechin. Snacks available from shop.

SPECIAL INFORMATION

Brechin Station is the only original Terminus station in preservation. The Bridge of Dun is also an original Victorian station. The Restaurant kitchen is the only full-length kitchen car in preservation.

OPERATING INFORMATION

Opening Times: Diesel service on Wednesdays in July and August. Open Easter Sunday, 3 Sundays before Christmas & every Sunday from June to September. Also open on a number of other dates for Special events.
Steam Working: Steam service on every Sunday from the end of May to 6th September.
Prices: Adult Return £4.50
Child Return £2.50
Family Return £14.00 (2 adult + 3 child)
Group discounts are available if booked in advance.

Detailed Directions by Car:
From South: For Brechin Station, leave the A90 at the Brechin turn-off and go straight through the Town Centre. Pass Amigos and the Northern Hotel, turn right at the T junction, it is then 150 yards to Park Road/St. Ninian Square; From North: For Brechin Station, leave the A90 at the Brechin turn-off and go straight through Trinity Village. Turn right at the mini-roundabout, it is then 250 yards to Park Road/St. Ninian Square. Bridge of Dun is situated half way between Brechin and Montrose.

CHASEWATER RAILWAY

Address: Brownhills West Station, Hednesford Road, Brownhills West, Walsall, West Midlands WS8 7LT	**Nº of Steam Locos:** 9
Telephone Nº: (01543) 452623	**Nº of Other Locos:** 6
Year Formed: 1985	**Nº of Members:** 350
Location of Line: Chasewater Park, Brownhills, near Walsall	**Annual Membership Fee:** Adult £7.50; Family £10.00; Concessions £5.00
Length of Line: 1½ miles	**Approx Nº of Visitors P.A.:** 7,500
	Gauge: Standard

GENERAL INFORMATION

Nearest Railtrack Station: Walsall or Birmingham (both approximately 8 miles)

Nearest Bus Station: Walsall or Birmingham

Car Parking: Free parking in Chasewater Park

Coach Parking: Free parking in Chasewater Park

Souvenir Shop(s): Yes

Food & Drinks: Yes

SPECIAL INFORMATION

Chasewater Railway is based on the Cannock Chase & Wolverhampton Railway opened in 1856, which passed into the hands of the National Coal Board which ceased using the line in 1965.

OPERATING INFORMATION

Opening Times: Sundays & Bank Holidays from Easter to October + Santa Specials.

Steam Working: First train at 12.00pm, then at 45 minute intervals until 5.15pm

Prices: Adult Return £1.95
Child Return 95p
Family Return £4.95

All tickets offer unlimited rides on the day of issue.

Detailed Directions by Car:

Chasewater Park is situated in Brownhills off the A5 southbound near the junction of the A5 with the A452 Chester Road.

CHINNOR & PRINCES RISBOROUGH RAILWAY

Address: Station Road, Chinnor, Oxon	**Nº of Steam Locos**: 1
Telephone Nº: (01844) 353535 (timetable)	**Nº of Other Locos**: 3
Year Formed: 1989	**Nº of Members**: 650
Location of Line: The Icknield Line, Princes Risborough	**Annual Membership Fee**: Adult £11.00; Family £16.50; Children & OAP £5.00
Length of Line: 3½ miles	**Approx Nº of Visitors P.A.**: 15,000
Gauge: Standard	

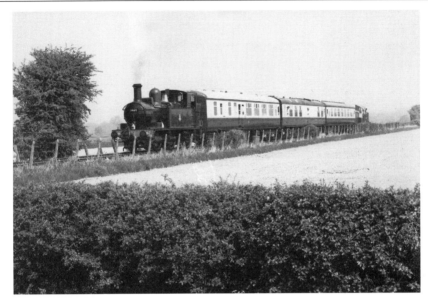

GENERAL INFORMATION

Nearest Railtrack Station: Princes Risborough (4 miles)
Nearest Bus Station: High Wycombe (10 miles)
Car Parking: Free parking at site
Coach Parking: Prior arrangement preferred but not necessary
Souvenir Shop(s): Yes
Food & Drinks: Soft drinks and light snacks in Station Buffet. 'Steam & Whistle Bar' is also open.

SPECIAL INFORMATION

The Chinnor & Princes Risborough Railway operates the remaining 3½ mile section of the former GWR Watlington Branch from Chinnor to Thame Junction.

OPERATING INFORMATION

Opening Times: Most Saturdays and all Sundays from Easter to October + Santa Specials.
Steam Working: 10.30am, 12.00pm, 1.30pm, 3.00pm and 4.30pm on most operating days.
Prices: Adult Return £5.00
 Child Return £3.00
 Family Return £13.00
  (2 adults + 2 children)
 Senior Citizen Return £4.00

Detailed Directions by Car:
From All Parts: The railway at Chinnor is situated in Station Road just off the B4009. Junction 6 of the M40 is 3 miles away and Princes Risborough 5 miles further along the B4009. Once in Chinnor follow the brown Tourist signs to the railway.

CHOLSEY & WALLINGFORD RAILWAY

Address: P.O. Box 16, St. John's Road, Wallingford, Oxon OX10 0NF	**N° of Steam Locos:** 1
Telephone N°: (01491) 835067 (24hr info)	**N° of Other Locos:** 4
Year Formed: 1981	**N° of Members:** 350
Location of Line: Wallingford, Oxon.	**Annual Membership Fee:** £10.00
Length of Line: 2½ miles	**Approx N° of Visitors P.A.:** 3,000
	Gauge: Standard

GENERAL INFORMATION

Nearest Railtrack Station: Joint station at Cholsey
Nearest Bus Station: Wallingford (1 mile)
Car Parking: Free parking available
Coach Parking: Free parking available
Souvenir Shop(s): Yes
Food & Drinks: Yes

SPECIAL INFORMATION

The Wallingford branch was originally intended as a through line to Princes Risborough, via Wallington, but ultimately became the first standard gauge branch of Brunel's broad-gauge London to Bristol line.

OPERATING INFORMATION

Opening Times: 2 day event (12th & 13th April) over Easter then May: 3rd, 4th, 24th & 25th; June: 7th & 21st; July: 5th & 19th; August: 9th, 30th & 31st; September: 13th & 27th; October: 17th & 18th. Also, Santa Specials on 6th, 13th, 19th & 20th December.
Steam Working: Approximately 11.30am to 5.00pm
Prices: Adult Return £3.50
Child Return £1.75
Family Return £9.50 (2 adults + 2 children)

Detailed Directions by Car:
From All Parts: Exit from the A34 at the Milton Interchange (between E. Ilsley and Abingdon). Follow signs to Didcot and Wallingford. Take Wallingford bypass, then turn left at the first roundabout (signposted Hithercroft Estate). The Station is ½ mile on the right by Pauls Maltings (prominent landmark which dominates the skyline).

CHURNET VALLEY RAILWAY

Address: The Railway Station, Cheddleton, Leek, Staffs. ST13 7EE
Telephone N°: (01538) 360522
Year Formed: 1978
Location of Line: Cheddleton
Length of Line: 1½ miles

N° of Steam Locos: 2
N° of Other Locos: 3
N° of Members: –
Annual Membership Fee: £9.00
Approx N° of Visitors P.A.: 20,000 plus
Gauge: Standard

GENERAL INFORMATION

Nearest Railtrack Station: Stoke-on-Trent (12 miles)
Nearest Bus Station: Leek (5 miles)
Car Parking: Parking available on site
Coach Parking: Restricted space – please book in advance
Souvenir Shop(s): Yes
Food & Drinks: Yes

SPECIAL INFORMATION

The Churnet Valley Railway is due to open a line extension to Consall in July 1998.

OPERATING INFORMATION

Opening Times: Trains run from 5th April until 5th October on all Sundays and Bank Holidays and most Saturdays.
Steam Working: 11.00am to 5.00pm
Prices: Please telephone (01538) 360522 for details.

Detailed Directions by Car:
From All Parts: Take the M6 to Stoke-on-Trent and follow trunk roads to Leek. The Railway is just off the A520 Leek to Stone road.

CLEETHORPES COAST LIGHT RAILWAY

Address: King's Road, Cleethorpes, North East Lincolnshire   DN35 0AG
Telephone Nº: (01472) 604657
Year Formed: 1948
Location of Line: Marine embankment along Cleethorpes seafront
Length of Line: 1 mile

Nº of Steam Locos: 6
Nº of Other Locos: 4
Nº of Members: 31
Annual Membership Fee: –
Approx Nº of Visitors P.A.: 96,000
Gauge: 15 inches

GENERAL INFORMATION

Nearest Railtrack Station: Cleethorpes (1 mile)
Nearest Bus Station: Sea Road (1 mile)
Car Parking: Boating Lake car park – 500 spaces (fee charged)
Coach Parking: As above
Souvenir Shop(s): Yes
Food & Drinks: Yes – Teapot Tearoom on Lakeside Station

SPECIAL INFORMATION

1998 will be the Railway's Golden Jubilee. A whole year of special events and openings are planned including a Steam Gala on 26th & 27th September.

OPERATING INFORMATION

Opening Times: Open daily from Easter until then end of September. Weekends only in the Winter. Open 11.00am to dusk in Winter, 6.30pm in Summer.
Steam Working: Easter until end September
Prices: Adult Return £1.50
Child Return £1.20
Family Return £4.50

Detailed Directions by Car:
Take the M180 to the A180 and continue to its' end. Follow signs for Cleethorpes. The Railway is situated along Cleethorpes seafront 1 mile south of the Pier. Look for the brown Railway Engine tourist signs.

COLNE VALLEY RAILWAY

Address: Castle Hedingham Station, Yeldham Road, Castle Hedingham, Essex, CO9 3DZ	**Length of Line**: 1 mile
	No of Steam Locos: 10
	No of Other Locos: 8
Telephone No: (01787) 461174	**No of Members**: 200
Year Formed: 1974	**Annual Membership Fee**: £11.00
Location of Line: On A1017, 7 miles north-west of Braintree	**Approx No of Visitors P.A.**: 40,000
	Gauge: Standard

GENERAL INFORMATION

Nearest Railtrack Station: Braintree (7 miles)
Nearest Bus Station: Hedingham bus from Braintree stops at the Railway (except on Sundays)
Car Parking: Free parking at site
Coach Parking: Free parking at site
Souvenir Shop(s): Yes
Food & Drinks: Yes – on operational days

SPECIAL INFORMATION

The railway was re-built on a section of the old Colne Valley & Halstead Railway, with all buildings, bridges, signal boxes, etc. re-located on site.

OPERATING INFORMATION

Opening Times: Trains run every Sunday and Bank Holiday from 22nd March to the end of October. Also Tuesdays, Wednesdays and Thursdays during the School Summer holidays. The Railway is open daily (sometimes without trains running) from 1st March to 23rd December 11.00am to 5.00pm.
Steam Working: Sundays 12.00pm to 4.00pm. Also Wednesdays & Thursdays in School summer holidays.
Prices: Adult – Steam days £5; Diesel days £4.00; Static days £2.00
Child – Steam £2.50; Diesel £2.00; Static £1.00
Family (2 adults + 4 children) – Steam £12.50; Diesel £10.00; Static £5.00

Detailed Directions by Car:
The Railway is situated on the A1017 between Halstead and Haverhill, 7 miles north-west of Braintree.

CONWY VALLEY RAILWAY MUSEUM

Address: Old Goods Yard, Betws-y-Coed, Gwynedd, North Wales LL24 0AL **Telephone N°:** (01690) 710568 **Year Formed:** 1983 **Location of Line:** Betws-y-Coed **Length of Line:** One and an eighth miles	**N° of Steam Locos:** 4 **N° of Other Locos:** 2 **N° of Members:** – **Annual Membership Fee:** – **Approx N° of Visitors P.A.:** 50,000 **Gauge:** 7¼ inches

GENERAL INFORMATION

Nearest Railtrack Station: Betws-y-Coed (20 yards)
Nearest Bus Station: 40 yards
Car Parking: Car park at site
Coach Parking: Car park at site
Souvenir Shop(s): Yes
Food & Drinks: Yes – Buffet Coach Cafe

SPECIAL INFORMATION

The Museum houses the unique 3D dioramas by the late Jack Nelson. Also the ¼ size steam loco 'Britannia'.

OPERATING INFORMATION

Opening Times: March to the end of October 10.15am to 5.30pm. Open in the Winter from 10.15am to 4.30pm weekends only.
Steam Working: Daily from 10.15am to 5.15pm
Prices: Adult – £1 entry to museum; Train 75p; Tram 60p
Child/OAP – 50p entry to museum; Train 75p; Tram 60p
Family tickets – £2.50

Detailed Directions by Car:
From Midlands & South: Take M54/M6 onto the A5 and into Betws-y-Coed; From Other Parts: Take the A55 coast road then the A407 to Betws-y-Coed. The museum is located by the Railtrack Station directly off the A5.

DARLINGTON RAILWAY CENTRE & MUSEUM

Address: North Road Station, Darlington, Co. Durham DL3 6ST	**Nº of Steam Locos**: 10
Telephone Nº: (01325) 460532	**Nº of Other Locos**: 8
Year Formed: 1975	**Nº of Members**: –
Location of Line: Adjacent to North Road Station	**Annual Membership Fee**: –
Length of Line: ¼ mile	**Approx Nº of Visitors P.A.**: 22,000
	Gauge: Standard

GENERAL INFORMATION

Nearest Railtrack Station: North Road (adjacent)
Nearest Bus Station: Darlington (1 mile)
Car Parking: Free parking at site
Coach Parking: Free parking at site
Souvenir Shop(s): Yes
Food & Drinks: Yes – Cafe in the Summer, drinks and confectionery at other times.

SPECIAL INFORMATION

The museum is an 1842 station on the route of the Stockton and Darlington Railway and is devoted to the Railways of north-east England.

OPERATING INFORMATION

Opening Times: The Museum is open 10.00am to 5.00pm daily, although it is closed during January. The Locomotive Works run by the A1 Steam Locomotive Trust is open 11.00am to 4.00pm on Saturdays.
Steam Working: Please enquire (selected dates only)
Prices: Adult – £2.10
Child – £1.05

Detailed Directions by Car:
From Darlington Town Centre: Follow the A167 north for about ¾ mile then turn left immediately before the Railway bridge; From A1(M): Exit at Junction 59 then follow A167 towards Darlington and turn right after passing under the Railway bridge.

DEAN FOREST RAILWAY

Address: Norchard Centre, Forest Road; Lydney, Gloucestershire GL15 4ET	**N° of Steam Locos:** 6
Telephone N°: (01594) 845840	**N° of Other Locos:** 4
Information Line: (01594) 843423 (24 hr.)	**N° of Members:** 750
Year Formed: 1970	**Annual Membership Fee:** Adult £12.00; Family (4 persons) £15.00
Location of Line: Lydney, Gloucestershire	**Approx N° of Visitors P.A.:** 55,000
Length of Line: 2 miles	**Gauge:** Standard

GENERAL INFORMATION

Nearest Railtrack Station: Lydney (200 metres)
Nearest Bus Station: Lydney (1 mile)
Car Parking: 600 spaces available (except on October 18th)
Coach Parking: Ample space (except October 18)
Souvenir Shop(s): Yes + a Museum
Food & Drinks: Yes – on operational days only

SPECIAL INFORMATION

Dean Forest Railway preserves the sole surviving line of the Severn and Wye Railway. The Railway is currently lengthening the line to a total of four miles – approximately half has been completed.

OPERATING INFORMATION

Opening Times: Sundays & Bank Holidays from Easter to 27th September. Also Wednesdays June to August and Tuesdays and Thursdays in August. Generally open from dawn until dusk.
Steam Working: Trains depart Norchard at 11.00am, 12.00pm, 1.30pm, 2.30pm, 3.30pm plus a 4.30pm departure on Sundays and Bank Holiday Saturday, Sunday and Mondays.
Prices: Adult Return £3.50
　　　　　Child Return £2.00
　　　　　Senior Citizens £3.00
Please note: Fares may differ on special dates.

Detailed Directions by Car:
From M50 & Ross-on-Wye: Take the B4228 and B4234 via Coleford to reach Lydney. Norchard is located on the B4234, ¾ mile north of Lydney Town Centre; From Monmouth: Take the A4136 and B4431 onto the B4234 via Coleford; From South Wales: Take the M4 then M48 onto the A48 via Chepstow to Lydney; From Midlands/Gloucester: Take the M5 to Gloucester then the A48 to Lydney.

Didcot Railway Centre

Address: Didcot Railway Centre, Didcot, Oxfordshire OX11 7NJ	**N° of Steam Locos**: 15
Telephone N°: (01235) 817200	**N° of Other Locos**: 2
Year Formed: 1962	**N° of Members**: 4,100
Location of Line: Didcot	**Annual Membership Fee**: Full £18.00;
Length of Line: ¾ mile	Over 60/Under 18 £10.00; Family £24.00
Gauge: Standard	**Approx N° of Visitors P.A.**: 70,000

GENERAL INFORMATION

Nearest Railtrack Station: Didcot Parkway (adjacent)
Nearest Bus Station: Buses to Didcot call at the Railway station
Car Parking: BR car park adjacent
Coach Parking: Further details on application
Souvenir Shop(s): Yes
Food & Drinks: Yes

SPECIAL INFORMATION

The Centre is based on a Great Western Railway engine shed and is devoted to the re-creation of part of the GWR.

OPERATING INFORMATION

Opening Times: Weekends all year round, open daily from 4th April to 27th September. 10.00am to 5.00pm (11.00am to 4.00pm in the Winter).
Steam Working: First & last Sundays of each month. Bank Holidays, all Sundays June to August, all Saturdays in August, all Wednesdays July to August.
Prices: Adult £4.00 – £6.50 (including rides)
Child £3.00 – £6.50 (including rides)
Discounted family tickets are often available (2 adults + 2 children).
Prices vary depending on the events.

Detailed Directions by Car:
From East & West: Take the M4 to Junction 13 then the A34 and A4130 (follow brown Tourist signs to Didcot Railway Centre); From North: The centre is signed from the A34 to A4130.

DOBWALLS FAMILY ADVENTURE PARK

Address: Dobwalls Family Adventure Park, near Liskeard, Cornwall PL14 6HD
Telephone Nº: (01579) 320325/321129
Information Line: (01579) 320578 (24 hr)
Year Formed: 1970
Location of Line: Near Liskeard, Cornwall
Length of Line: 2 × 1 mile tracks

Nº of Steam Locos: 6
Nº of Other Locos: 4
Nº of Members: –
Annual Membership Fee: –
Approx Nº of Visitors P.A.: 350,000
Gauge: 7¼ inches

GENERAL INFORMATION

Nearest Railtrack Station: Liskeard (3 miles)
Nearest Bus Station: Most National Express Coaches travel through Dobwalls.
Car Parking: Ample parking available at site
Coach Parking: Large coach park available
Souvenir Shop(s): Yes
Food & Drinks: Yes

SPECIAL INFORMATION

Formerly known as the Forest Railroad Park, Dobwalls has a large number of other attractions including many for children. There is also a craft centre and art gallery.

OPERATING INFORMATION

Opening Times: Daily from Easter to the End of September 10.30am to 5.00pm. Often opens earlier and closes later during the Peak season.
Steam Working: All days when open
Prices: Children under the age of 3 – Free
Children ages 6 to 11 – £5.99
Ages 12 to 60 – £5.50
Ages 60 and over – £4.99
Disabled – £3.80
Family Ticket £19.00 (2 adult + 2 children)

Detailed Directions by Car:
From All Parts: Dobwalls Family Adventure Park is situated just off the A38 at Dobwalls village, 3 miles from Liskeard.

EAST ANGLIAN RAILWAY MUSEUM

Address: Chappel & Wakes Colne Station, Colchester, Essex CO6 2DS	**N⁰ of Steam Locos:** 7
Telephone N⁰: (01206) 242524	**N⁰ of Other Locos:** 6
Year Formed: 1969	**N⁰ of Members:** 750
Location of Line: 8 miles south of Colchester on Marks Tey to Sudbury branch	**Annual Membership Fee:** Adult £14.00; Senior Citizen £9.00
Length of Line: A third of a mile	**Approx N⁰ of Visitors P.A.:** 40,000
	Gauge: Standard

GENERAL INFORMATION

Nearest Railtrack Station: Chappel & Wakes Colne (adajcent)
Nearest Bus Station: Chappel (500 yards)
Car Parking: Free parking at site
Coach Parking: Free parking at site
Souvenir Shop(s): Yes
Food & Drinks: Yes – all weekends & every day in the summer.

SPECIAL INFORMATION

The museum has the most comprehensive collection of railway architecture & engineering in the region.

OPERATING INFORMATION

Opening Times: Open daily 10.00am to 4.30pm. Steam days open from 11.00am to 5.00pm
Steam Working: Steam days are the 1st Sunday monthly from April to August and also in October. Bank Holidays are also Steam days.
Prices: Adult £2.50 non-Steam; £4.50 Steam
  Child £1.50 non-Steam; £2.50 Steam
  O.A.P. £2.00 non-Steam; £3.50 Steam
  Family £7.50 non-Steam; £13.00 Steam
Children under the age of 4 are admitted free of charge. A 10% discount is available for bookings for more than 10 people.

Detailed Directions by Car:
From North & South: Turn off the A12 south west of Colchester onto the A1124 (formerly the A604). The Museum is situated just off the A1124; From West: Turn off the A120 just before Marks Tey (signposted).

EAST LANCASHIRE RAILWAY

Address: Bolton Street Station, Bury, Lancashire   BL9 0EY
Telephone Nº: (0161) 764-7790
Year Formed: 1968
Location of Line: Bury to Rawtenstall
Length of Line: 8 miles

Nº of Steam Locos: 20
Nº of Other Locos: 19
Nº of Members: 3,000
Annual Membership Fee: £10.00
Approx Nº of Visitors P.A.: 120,000
Gauge: Standard

GENERAL INFORMATION

Nearest Railtrack Station: Manchester (then Metro Link to Bury)
Nearest Bus Station: ¼ mile
Car Parking: Adjacent
Coach Parking: Adjacent
Souvenir Shop(s): Yes
Food & Drinks: Yes

SPECIAL INFORMATION

Originally opened in 1846, the East Lancashire Railway was re-opened in 1991.

OPERATING INFORMATION

Opening Times: Every weekend & Bank Holiday 10.00am to 4.00pm
Steam Working: Most trains are steam-hauled (Saturdays alternate Steam & Diesel)
Prices: Adult Return £6.00
Child Return £4.00
Family Return 16.00
Cheaper fares are available for shorter journeys.

Detailed Directions by Car:
From All Parts: Exit the M66 at Junction 2 and take the A56 into Bury. Follow the brown tourist signs and turn right into Bolton Street at the junction with the A58. The station is about 150 yards on the right.

EAST SOMERSET RAILWAY

Address: Cranmore Railway Station, Shepton Mallet, Somerset BA4 4QP	**N° of Steam Locos**: Between 3 and 5
Telephone N°: (01749) 880417	**N° of Other Locos**: 1
Year Formed: 1971	**N° of Members**: 450
Location of Line: Cranmore, off A361 between Frome & Shepton Mallet	**Annual Membership Fee**: Single £8.00; Couple £10.00; Family £15.00
Length of Line: 2 miles	**Approx N° of Visitors P.A.**: 25,000
	Gauge: Standard

GENERAL INFORMATION

Nearest Railtrack Station: Castle Cary (10 miles)
Nearest Bus Station: Shepton Mallet (3 miles)
Car Parking: Space for 100 cars available
Coach Parking: Available by arrangement
Souvenir Shop(s): Yes
Food & Drinks: Yes

SPECIAL INFORMATION

Footplate experience courses available – phone (01749) 880417 for further details.

OPERATING INFORMATION

Opening Times: Sundays in the Winter, weekends in March, April & October, weekdays in the Summer. Open daily in August and September. Santa Specials run on weekends in December. Other special events run on various dates. Open 10.00am to 4.00pm in the Winter, 10.00am to 5.30pm in the Summer.
Steam Working: All operating days.
Prices: Adult £5.50
            Child £3.50
            Senior Citizens £4.50
            Family £15.00

Detailed Directions by Car:
From North: Take A367/A37 to Shepton Mallet then turn left onto A361 to Frome. Carry on to Shepton Mallet and 9 miles after Frome turn left at Cranmore; From South: Take A36 to Frome bypass then A361 to Cranmore; From West: Take A371 from Wells to Shepton Mallet, then A361 to Frome (then as above).

EMBSAY & BOLTON ABBEY STEAM RAILWAY

Address: Embsay Station, Embsay, Skipton, N. Yorkshire BD23 6QX	**N⁰ of Steam Locos:** 21
Telephone N⁰: (01756) 794727	**N⁰ of Other Locos:** 11
Year Formed: 1968	**N⁰ of Members:** 700
Location of Line: 2 miles east of Skipton	**Annual Membership Fee:** £8.00
Length of Line: 4½ miles	**Approx N⁰ of Visitors P.A.:** 88,000
	Gauge: Standard

GENERAL INFORMATION

Nearest Railtrack Station: Skipton (2 miles)
Nearest Bus Station: Skipton (2 miles)
Car Parking: Large car park at both Stations
Coach Parking: Large coach park at both Stations
Souvenir Shop(s): Yes
Food & Drinks: Yes – Cafe + Buffet cars

SPECIAL INFORMATION

An extension of the line to Bolton Abbey has now opened.

OPERATING INFORMATION

Opening Times: Trains run every Sunday throughout the year and on Tuesdays & Saturdays in July and September. Daily (but for Mondays and Fridays) from 18th July to the end of August. Trains also run on Bank Holidays and on some other dates.
Steam Working: Trains depart Embsay Station at 10.45am, 12.15pm, 1.40pm, 3.05pm & 4.25pm during the Main Season. During the Winter (until 22nd March 1998 and from 25th October 1998) trains run at 10.45am, 12.25pm, 1.55pm & 3.20 pm.
Prices: Adult Return £4.50
Child Return £2.00
Different fares may apply on special event days.

Detailed Directions by Car:
From All Parts: Embsay Station is off the A59 Skipton bypass by the Harrogate Road. Bolton Abbey Station is off the A59 at Bolton Abbey.

FAIRBOURNE & BARMOUTH RAILWAY

Address: Beach Road, Fairbourne, Dolgellau, Gwynedd   LL38 2PZ
Telephone Nº: (01341) 250362
Year Formed: 1947
Location of Line: On A493 between Tywyn & Dolgellau
Length of Line: 2½ miles

Nº of Steam Locos: 4
Nº of Other Locos: 2
Nº of Members: 12
Annual Membership Fee: £6.00
Approx Nº of Visitors P.A.: 25,000
Gauge: 12¼ inches

GENERAL INFORMATION

Nearest Railtrack Station: Fairbourne (adjacent)
Nearest Bus Station: Fairbourne (adjacent)
Car Parking: Free parking in Railtrack car park
Coach Parking: Pay & Display car park 300 yards (the Railway will re-imburse car parking charges for party bookings)
Souvenir Shop(s): Yes
Food & Drinks: Yes – Tea room at Fairbourne, Cafe at Porth Penrhyn Terminus

SPECIAL INFORMATION

There is a connecting ferry service (passenger only) to Barmouth from Porth Penrhyn Terminus.

OPERATING INFORMATION

Opening Times: Operates on 5th to 19th and also 25th & 26th April. Then opens from 2nd May to 27th September. Also opens on 18th October to 1st November and and December 12th & 13th.
Steam Working: 10.45am to 4.20pm on operating days.
Prices: Adult £3.80
Child £2.40
Family £11.00 (2 adults + up to 3 children)

Detailed Directions by Car:
From North & East Wales: Follow Dolgellau signs, turn left onto A493 towards Tywyn. The turn-off for Fairbourne is located 9 miles south west of Dolgellau; From South Wales: Follow signs for Machynlleth, then follow A487 towards Dolgellau. Then take A493 towards Fairbourne.

FFESTINIOG RAILWAY

Address: Ffestiniog Railway, Harbour Station, Porthmadog, Gwynedd LL49 9NF	**Length of Line:** 13½ miles
Telephone Nº: (01766) 512340	**Nº of Steam Locos:** 12
Web Site: http://www.festrail.co.uk	**Nº of Other Locos:** 12
Year Formed: 1832	**Nº of Members:** 5,000
Location of Line: Porthmadog to Blaenau Ffestiniog	**Annual Membership Fee:** –
	Approx Nº of Visitors P.A.: 200,000
	Gauge: 1 foot 11½ inches

GENERAL INFORMATION

Nearest Railtrack Station: Porthmadog (1 mile)
Nearest Bus Station: Bus stop next to stations at Porthmadog & Blaenau Ffestiniog
Car Parking: Parking available at Porthmadog & Blaenau Ffestiniog
Coach Parking: Available at Porthmadog & Blaenau Ffestiniog
Souvenir Shop(s): Yes
Food & Drinks: Yes

SPECIAL INFORMATION

The Railway runs through the spectacular scenery of Snowdonia National Park. The Ffestiniog Railway also operates the newly opened three mile Rheilffordd Eryn – Welsh Highland Railway at Caernarfon.

OPERATING INFORMATION

Opening Times: Daily service from the end of March to early November. Limited service in the Winter. Train times vary.
Steam Working: Most trains are steam hauled. Limited in the Winter, however.
Prices: Adult £12.80
Child £6.40 (1 child free with each adult)
Reductions are available for Senior Citizens and groups of 20 or more.

Detailed Directions by Car:
Portmadog is easily accessible from the Midlands – take the M54/A5 to Corwen then the A494 to Bala onto the A4212 to Trawsfynydd and the A470 (becomes the A487 from Maentwrog) to Porthmadog. From Chester take the A55 to Llandudno Junction and the A470 to Blaenau Ffestiniog. Both Stations are well-signposted.

FOXFIELD LIGHT RAILWAY

Address: Caverswall Road Station, Blythe Bridge, Stoke-on-Trent, Staffs. ST11 9EA
Telephone Nº: (01782) 396210
Year Formed: 1967
Location of Line: Blythe Bridge
Length of Line: 3½ miles
Gauge: Standard

Nº of Steam Locos: 16
Nº of Other Locos: 15
Nº of Members: Over 300
Annual Membership Fee: Adult £8.00; Junior £5.00; Family £12.00
Approx Nº of Visitors P.A.: 25,000

GENERAL INFORMATION

Nearest Railtrack Station: Blythe Bridge (¼ mile)
Nearest Bus Station: Hanley (5 miles)
Car Parking: Space for 300 cars available
Coach Parking: Space for 6 coaches available
Souvenir Shop(s): Yes
Food & Drinks: Yes – with a bar on the trains

SPECIAL INFORMATION

The Railway is a former Colliery railway built in 1893 to take coal from Foxfield Colliery. It has the steepest Standard Gauge adhesion worked gradient in the UK.

OPERATING INFORMATION

Opening Times: Sundays & Bank Holiday Mondays from Easter to the end of September. Also weekends in December. Open 10.30am to 5.00pm.
Steam Working: 11.30am, 1.00pm, 2.00pm. 3.00pm & 4.00pm
Prices: Adult £3.90
Child £1.80
Family £10.00 (2 adults + 2 children or 1 adult + 4 children)
Fares may vary on special event days.

Detailed Directions by Car:
From South: Exit M6 at Junction 14 onto the A34 to Stone then the A520 to Meir and the A50 to Blythe Bridge; From North: Exit M6 at Junction 15 then the A500 to Stoke-on-Trent and the A50 to Blythe Bridge; From East: Take the A50 to Blythe Bridge. Once in Blythe Bridge, turn by the Railtrack crossing.

GLOUCESTER & WARWICKSHIRE RAILWAY

Address: The Station, Toddington,
Cheltenham, Gloucestershire   GL54 5DT
Telephone Nº: (01242) 621405
Year Formed: 1981
Location of Line: 5 miles south of
Broadway, Worcestershire, near the A46
Length of Line: 6½ miles

Nº of Steam Locos: 9
Nº of Other Locos: 15
Nº of Members: 2,000
Annual Membership Fee: −
Approx Nº of Visitors P.A.: 50,000
Gauge: Both Standard and Narrow Gauge

GENERAL INFORMATION

Nearest Railtrack Station: Cheltenham Spa or
Ashchurch
Nearest Bus Station: Cheltenham
Car Parking: Parking available at Toddington and
Winchcombe Stations
Coach Parking: Parking available as above
Souvenir Shop(s): Yes
Food & Drinks: Yes

SPECIAL INFORMATION

The Railway has both Standard & Narrow gauge in
operation.

OPERATING INFORMATION

Opening Times: Weekends & Bank Holidays. Also
daily during School Summer Holidays. 10.00am to
5.00pm
Steam Working: Operating days
Prices: Adult Return £6.00
             Child Return £4.00

Detailed Directions by Car:
Toddington is 11 miles north east of Cheltenham, 5 miles south of Broadway just off the B4632 (old A46). The
Railway is clearly visible from the B4632.

GREAT CENTRAL RAILWAY

Address: Loughborough Central Station, Great Central Road, Loughborough, Leicestershire LE11 1RW	**Length of Line**: 8 miles
	N⁰ of Steam Locos: 21
	N⁰ of Other Locos: 9
Telephone N⁰: (01509) 230726	**N⁰ of Members**: 5,000
Year Formed: 1969	**Annual Membership Fee**: £15.00
Location of Line: From Loughborough to Leicester	**Approx N⁰ of Visitors P.A.**: 150,000
	Gauge: Standard

GENERAL INFORMATION

Nearest Railtrack Station: Loughborough (1 mile)
Nearest Bus Station: Loughborough (¼ mile)
Car Parking: Street parking in Loughborough
Coach Parking: Car parks at Quorn & Woodhouse and Rothley
Souvenir Shop(s): Yes
Food & Drinks: Yes – Buffet or Restaurant cars are usually available for snacks or other meals

SPECIAL INFORMATION

The aim of the GCR is to recreate the experience of British main line railway operation during the best years of steam locomotives.

OPERATING INFORMATION

Opening Times: Open daily throughout the year.
Steam Working: Weekends and Bank Holidays throughout the year. Also weekdays in the Summer.
Prices: Adult Return £8.00
Child/Senior Citizen Return £5.25
Family Ticket £17.50 (2 adult + 3 children)

Detailed Directions by Car:
Great Central Road is on the South East side of Loughborough and is clearly signposted from the A6 Leicester Road and A60 Nottingham Road.

GREAT NORTHERN RAILWAY

Address: The Railway Station, Ludborough, Lincolnshire DN36 5SQ	**N° of Steam Locos:** 2
Telephone N°: (01507) 363881	**N° of Other Locos:** 2
Year Formed: 1981	**N° of Members:** Approximately 200
Location of Line: Ludborough – off the A16(T) between Grimsby and Louth	**Annual Membership Fee:** £10.00
Length of Line: ½ mile	**Approx N° of Visitors P.A.:** 1,000

GENERAL INFORMATION

Nearest Railtrack Station: Grimsby (8 miles)
Nearest Bus Stop: Ludborough (½ mile)
Car Parking: 100 spaces for cars at the Station
Coach Parking: Space for 1 coach only
Souvenir Shop(s): Yes
Food & Drinks: Yes

SPECIAL INFORMATION

The buildings and facilities at Ludborough are now virtually completed and short steam trips should commence in 1998. Plans to extend the line to North Thoresby (1 mile) are being considered.

OPERATING INFORMATION

Opening Times: Summer weekends and Bank Holidays.
Steam Working: 10.00am to 3.30pm
Prices: Adult £1.00
         Child 50p

Detailed Directions by Car:
The Railway is situated in Ludborough, ½ mile off the A16(T) Louth to Grimsby road. Follow the signs to Fulstow to reach the station.

GWILI RAILWAY

Address: Bronwydd Arms Station, Bronwydd Arms, Carmarthen SA33 6HT	**Nº of Steam Locos**: 8
Telephone Nº: (01267) 230666	**Nº of Other Locos**: 11
Year Formed: 1975	**Nº of Members**: 900 shareholders, 500 Society members
Location of Line: Near Carmarthen, South Wales	**Annual Membership Fee**: £10.00
	Approx Nº of Visitors P.A.: 18,000
Length of Line: 1.6 miles currently in use	**Gauge**: Standard

GENERAL INFORMATION

Nearest Railtrack Station: Carmarthen (3 miles)
Nearest Bus Station: Carmarthen (3 miles)
Car Parking: Free parking at Bronwydd Arms except for a few special occasions
Coach Parking: Free parking at Bronwydd Arms
Souvenir Shop(s): Yes
Food & Drinks: Yes

SPECIAL INFORMATION

Gwili Railway was the first Standard Gauge preserved railway in Wales. There is a riverside picnic area at the end of the line.

OPERATING INFORMATION

Opening Times: Daily from July 25th to September 1st. Also open Wednesdays and Sundays in May, June & July and various other times during school holidays. Please phone for further details.
Steam Working: Most advertised trains are steam hauled. Trains run from 11.30am to 4.00pm.
Prices: Adult £3.50
          Child £2.00
          Family £9.00 (2 adults + up to 3 children)
          Senior Citizens £2.00

Detailed Directions by Car:
The Railway is three miles North of Carmarthen – signposted off the A484 Carmarthen to Cardigan Road.

HOLLYCOMBE STEAM COLLECTION

Address: Hollycombe House, near Liphook, Hants. GU30 7LP	½ mile Standard gauge
Telephone N°: (01428) 724900	**N° of Steam Locos:** 2
Year Formed: 1970	**N° of Other Locos:** –
Location of Line: In the grounds of Hollycombe House	**N° of Members:** 50
	Annual Membership Fee: £7.00
Length of Line: 1¾ miles Narrow gauge,	**Approx N° of Visitors P.A.:** 25,000
	Gauge: 2 feet (narrow gauge)

GENERAL INFORMATION

Nearest Railtrack Station: Liphook (2 miles)
Nearest Bus Station: Liphook
Car Parking: Extensive grass area may be used
Coach Parking: Hardstanding for several
Souvenir Shop(s): Yes
Food & Drinks: Yes – Cafe

SPECIAL INFORMATION

The narrow gauge railway ascends to spectacular views of the Downs.

OPERATING INFORMATION

Opening Times: Sundays from Good Friday & Bank Holiday Mondays. Open daily from 26th to 31st July and from 16th to 31st August.
Steam Working: 2.00pm to 6.00pm
Prices: Adult £5.50
Child £4.50
Family £17.00 (2 adults + 2 children)

Detailed Directions by Car:
Follow the A3 to Liphook and then follow the brown tourist signs.

ISLE OF MAN RAILWAYS

Address: Strathallan Crescent, Douglas, Isle of Man IM2 4NR	**Nº of Steam Locos:** 5
Telephone Nº: (01624) 663366	**Nº of Other Locos:** 2
Year Formed: 1873	**Nº of Members:** –
Location of Line: Douglas to Port Erin	**Annual Membership Fee:** –
Length of Line: 15½ miles	**Approx Nº of Visitors P.A.:** 100,000
	Gauge: 3 feet

GENERAL INFORMATION

Nearest Railtrack Station: Not applicable
Nearest Bus Station: Douglas
Car Parking: Limited parking at all stations
Coach Parking: Available at Douglas & Port Erin
Souvenir Shop(s): Yes – at Douglas Station and Port Erin Railway Museum
Food & Drinks: Yes – at Douglas & Port Erin stations

SPECIAL INFORMATION

Steam 125 Celebrations during 1998: Enthusiasts week from 2nd to 9th May 1998; Gala Fortnight from 27th June to 11th July; Summer Spectacular from 15th to 23rd August.

OPERATING INFORMATION

Opening Times: From Easter to 4th October. Then again for the final week of October.
Steam Working: As above
Prices: Adult Day Return £7.20; 3 Day Rail-Rover £15.20
Child Day Return £3.60; 3 Day Rail-Rover £7.60
Accompanied children – pay for the first two children, the next two travel free of charge.

Detailed Directions by Car:
Ferry from Heysham (Lancashire) or Liverpool to reach Isle of Man. Douglas Station is ½ mile inland from the Ferry terminal and promenade (fully signposted).

ISLE OF WIGHT STEAM RAILWAY

Address: The Railway Station, Haven Street, Ryde, Isle of Wight PO33 4DS	**Nº of Steam Locos:** 6
Telephone Nº: (01983) 882204	**Nº of Other Locos:** 3
Year Formed: 1971	**Nº of Members:** 1,300
Location of Line: Between Ryde & Wootton	**Annual Membership Fee:** £15.00
Length of Line: 5 miles	**Approx Nº of Visitors P.A.:** 100,000
	Gauge: Standard

GENERAL INFORMATION

Nearest Railtrack Station: Smallbrook Junction (direct interchange)
Nearest Bus Station: Ryde (3 miles)
Car Parking: Free parking at Havenstreet & Wootton Stations
Coach Parking: Free at Havenstreet Station
Souvenir Shop(s): Yes – at Havenstreet Station
Food & Drinks: Yes – at Havenstreet Station

SPECIAL INFORMATION

The IWSR uses mostly Victorian & Edwardian locomotives and carriages to recreate the atmosphere of an Isle of Wight branch line railway.

OPERATING INFORMATION

Opening Times: 26th March to 29th October. Open selected days & bank holidays. Open daily from 23rd May to 27th September.
Steam Working: 10.30am to 4.00pm (depending on the Station)
Prices: Adult Return £6.00
Child Return £4.00
Family Return £19.00
(2 adults + 2 children)

Detailed Directions by Car:
To reach the Isle of Wight head for the Ferry ports at Lymington, Southampton or Portsmouth. From all parts of the Isle of Wight, head for Ryde and follow the brown tourist signs.

KEIGHLEY & WORTH VALLEY RAILWAY

Address: The Station, Haworth, Keighley, West Yorkshire BD22 8NJ
Telephone Nº: (01535) 645214 (Enquiries); (01535) 647777 (24 hour timetable)
Year Formed: 1962 (Line re-opened 1968)
Location of Line: From Keighley southwards through Haworth to Oxenhope
Length of Line: 4¾ miles

Nº of Steam Locos: 30
Nº of Other Locos: 10
Members: 4,500 (350 working members)
Annual Membership Fee: Adult £12.00; Adult life membership £240.
Approx Nº of Visitors P.A.: 150,000
Gauge: Standard
Web Site: http://www.kwvr.co.uk

GENERAL INFORMATION

Nearest Railtrack Station: Keighley (adjacent)
Nearest Bus Station: Keighley (5 minutes walk)
Car Parking: Parking at Keighley, Ingrow, Haworth (charged) and Oxenhope
Coach Parking: At Ingrow & Oxenhope (phone in advance)
Souvenir Shop(s): Yes – at Keighley, Haworth & Oxenhope
Food & Drinks: Yes – at Keighley & Oxenhope when trains run.

OPERATING INFORMATION

Opening Times: Weekends & Bank Holidays throughout the year. Daily from June 20th to September 6th. Also open during Easter and 26th December to 1st January.
Steam Working: Early trains are Diesel; Steam runs from mid-morning on all operating days (except 4 weekends prior to Christmas).
Prices: Adult Return £5.20; £6.50 day rover
Child Return £2.50; £3.25 day rover
Family Return £13.00 (2 Adults, 3 children); £15.00 Family day rover

---

Detailed Directions by Car:
Exit the M62 at Junction 26 and take the M606 to its' end. Follow the ring-road signs around Bradford to Shipley. Take the A650 through Bingley to Keighley and follow the brown tourist signs to the railway. Alternatively, take the A6033 from Hebden Bridge to Oxenhope and follow the brown signs to Oxenhope or Haworth Stations.

KENT & EAST SUSSEX RAILWAY

Address: Tenterden Town Station, Tenterden, Kent   TN30 6HE
Telephone Nº: (01580) 765155
Year Formed: 1973
Location of Line: Tenterden, Kent to Northiam, East Sussex
Length of Line: 7 miles

Nº of Steam Locos: 12
Nº of Other Locos: 6
Nº of Members: 3,000
Annual Membership Fee: £12.00
Approx Nº of Visitors P.A.: 85,000
Gauge: Standard

GENERAL INFORMATION

Nearest Railtrack Station: Headcorn (10 miles)
Nearest Bus Station: Tenterden
Car Parking: Parking at Tenderden Town & Northiam Stations
Coach Parking: As above
Souvenir Shop(s): Yes
Food & Drinks: Yes

SPECIAL INFORMATION

Built as Britain's first light railway, the K&ESR opened in 1900 and was epitomised by sharp curved and steep gradients and to this day retains a charm and atmosphere all of its own.

OPERATING INFORMATION

Opening Times: March – Sundays only; April to October – weekends, bank holidays and school holidays; June and September – every day but Mondays and Fridays (although open on 4th & 7th September); Daily in July and August; Santa specials at weekends in December and the week before Christmas.
Steam Working: Every operational day
Prices: Adult £6.50
             Child £3.25
             Family £17.50

Detailed Directions by Car:
From London and Kent Coast: Travel to Ashford (M20) then take the A28 to Tenterden; From Sussex Coast: Take A28 from Hastings to Northiam.

KIRKLEES LIGHT RAILWAY

Address: Park Mill Way, Clayton West,
near Huddersfield, W. Yorks.   HD8 9XJ
Telephone Nº: (01484) 865727
Year Formed: 1991
Location of Line: Clayton West to Shelley
Length of Line: 4 miles

Nº of Steam Locos: 3
Nº of Other Locos: 1
Nº of Members: –
Annual Membership Fee: –
Approx Nº of Visitors P.A.: –
Gauge: 15 inches

GENERAL INFORMATION

Nearest Railtrack Station: Denby Dale (4 miles)
Nearest Bus Station: Bus stop outside gates. Take 484 from Wakefield or 235 from Huddersfield/Barnsley.
Car Parking: Ample free parking at site
Coach Parking: Ample free parking at site
Souvenir Shop(s): Yes
Food & Drinks: Yes

SPECIAL INFORMATION

The opening of a new station & visitor centre is planned for Spring 1998.

OPERATING INFORMATION

Opening Times: Open every weekend and most school holidays in the Winter. Open daily from Spring bank holiday to the end of August.
Steam Working: All trains are steam-hauled. Trains run hourly from 11.00am
Prices: Please phone for details

Detailed Directions by Car:
The Railway is located on the A636 Wakefield to Denby Dale road. Turn off the M1 at Junction 38 and the railway is 4 miles.

LAKESIDE & HAVERTHWAITE RAILWAY

Address: Haverthwaite Station, near Ulverston, Cumbria   LA12 8AL
Telephone Nº: (01539) 531594
Year Formed: 1973
Location of Line: Haverthwaite to Lakeside
Length of Line: 3½ miles

Nº of Steam Locos: 6
Nº of Other Locos: 6
Nº of Members: 250
Annual Membership Fee: –
Approx Nº of Visitors P.A.: 170,000
Gauge: Standard

GENERAL INFORMATION
Nearest Railtrack Station: Ulverston (7 miles)
Nearest Bus Station: Haverthwaite (100 yards)
Car Parking: Plenty of spaces – 50p charge
Coach Parking: Free parking at site
Souvenir Shop(s): Yes
Food & Drinks: Yes

SPECIAL INFORMATION
Connections are available at Lakeside for Windermere Lake Cruises to Bowness & Ambleside. Through tickets are available.

OPERATING INFORMATION
Opening Times: Daily from April 4th to April 19th and May 2nd to November 1st. Also open 25th & 26th April.
Steam Working: Daily from morning to late afternoon.
Prices: Adult Return £3.40; Single £2.00
Child Return £1.70; Single £1.30

Detailed Directions by Car:
From All Parts: Exit the M6 at Junction 36 and follow the brown tourist signs.

LAPPA VALLEY STEAM RAILWAY

Address: St. Newlyn East, Newquay, Cornwall TR8 5HZ	**Nº of Steam Locos:** 2
Telephone Nº: (01872) 510317	**Nº of Other Locos:** 2
Year Formed: 1974	**Nº of Members:** –
Location of Line: Benny Halt to East Wheal Rose, near St. Newlyn East	**Annual Membership Fee:** –
	Approx Nº of Visitors P.A.: 45,000
Length of Line: 1 mile	**Gauge:** 15 inches

GENERAL INFORMATION

Nearest Railtrack Station: Newquay (5 miles)
Nearest Bus Station: Newquay (5 miles)
Car Parking: Free parking at Benny Halt
Coach Parking: Free parking at Benny Halt
Souvenir Shop(s): Yes
Food & Drinks: Yes

SPECIAL INFORMATION

The railway runs on part of the former Newquay to Chacewater branch line. Site also has a Grade II listed mine building, boating, play areas for children and 2 other miniature train rides.

OPERATING INFORMATION

Opening Times: Open daily from 5th April to 1st October and from 24th to 30th October. Also open on Sundays, Tuesdays, Wednesdays and Thursdays in October.
Steam Working: 10.30am to 4.30pm or later on operating days
Prices: Adult £5.80
Child £3.30
Family £16.80 (2 adults + 2 children)

Detailed Directions by Car:
The railway is signposted from the A30 at the Summercourt-Mitchell bypass, from the A3075 south of Newquay and the A3058 east of Newquay.

LAUNCESTON STEAM RAILWAY

Address: Launceston, Cornwall PL15 8DA	**N⁰ of Steam Locos:** 5 (3 working)
Telephone N⁰: (01566) 775665	**N⁰ of Other Locos:** None
Year Formed: Opened in 1983	**N⁰ of Members:** –
Location of Line: Launceston to Newmills	**Annual Membership Fee:** –
Length of Line: 2¼ miles	**Gauge:** 60 centimetres

GENERAL INFORMATION

Nearest Railtrack Station: Liskeard (15 miles)
Nearest Bus Station: Launceston (½ mile) – very infrequent service however
Car Parking: At Station, Newport Industrial Estate, Launceston
Coach Parking: As above
Souvenir Shop(s): Yes – also with a bookshop
Food & Drinks: Yes – Cafe, snacks & drinks

SPECIAL INFORMATION

During the Summer school holidays, two engines are sometimes in operation.

OPERATING INFORMATION

Opening Times: Good Friday to Easter Monday inclusive, then Sundays & Tuesdays only until Whitsun. Then daily (except Saturdays) until the end of September. Open Sundays & Tuesdays in October and weekend afternoons in December.
Steam Working: 11.00am to 4.30pm on operational days
Prices: Adult £5.20
Child £3.50
Family £16.80 (2 adults + 4 children)
Senior Citizen £4.70
Group rates are available upon application.
These prices include as many trips as you like on the day of purchase.

Detailed Directions by Car:
Drive to Launceston and look for the brown Steam Engine Tourist signs. Use the L.S.R. car park at the Newport Industrial Estate.

THE LAVENDER LINE

Address: Isfield Station, Isfield, near Uckfield, East Sussex TN22 5XB
Telephone Nº: (01825) 750515
Year Formed: 1992
Location of Line: East Sussex between Lewes and Uckfield
Length of Line: ¾ mile

Nº of Steam Locos: 2
Nº of Other Locos: 1
Nº of Members: Approximately 350
Annual Membership Fee: £10.00
Approx Nº of Visitors P.A.: 12,000

GENERAL INFORMATION

Nearest Railtrack Station: Uckfield (3 miles)
Nearest Bus Station: Uckfield (3 miles)
Car Parking: Free parking at site
Coach Parking: Can cater for coach parties – please contact the Railway.
Souvenir Shop(s): Yes
Food & Drinks: Yes – Cinders Buffet

SPECIAL INFORMATION

Uckfield Station has been restored as a Southern Railway country station complete with the original L.B.S.C.R. signalbox.

OPERATING INFORMATION

Opening Times: Sundays throughout the year. Saturdays and Sundays in July and August. Also open on Bank Holidays and in December for Santa Specials.
Steam Working: Throughout the operating days.
Prices: Adult £3.50
Child £2.00
Senior Citizen £2.00
Family (2 adults + 2 children) £9.50
All tickets offer unlimited rides on the day of issue.

Detailed Directions by Car:
From All Parts: Isfield is just off the A26 midway between Lewes and Uckfield.

LEIGHTON BUZZARD RAILWAY

Address: Pages Park Station, Billington Road, Leighton Buzzard, Beds. LU7 8TN
Telephone Nº: (01525) 373888
Year Formed: 1967
Location of Line: Leighton Buzzard
Length of Line: 3 miles

Nº of Steam Locos: 11
Nº of Other Locos: 39
Nº of Members: 340
Annual Membership Fee: £13.00
Approx Nº of Visitors P.A.: 15,000
Gauge: 2 feet

GENERAL INFORMATION

Nearest Railtrack Station: Leighton Buzzard (2 miles)
Nearest Bus Station: Leighton Buzzard (¾ mile)
Car Parking: Free parking adjacent
Coach Parking: Free parking adjacent
Souvenir Shop(s): Yes
Food & Drinks: Yes

SPECIAL INFORMATION

There are a number of special events schedules throughout the year. Please contact the Railway for further information.

OPERATING INFORMATION

Opening Times: Sundays from mid-March to mid-October and also in December. Open on bank holidays and in August (except for Mondays and Fridays). Also open on some Saturdays and Mondays throughout the year. Trains run from mid-morning to late afternoon.
Steam Working: Most operating days.
Prices: Adult £4.50
Child £1.50
Senior Citizens £3.50

Detailed Directions by Car:
The railway is 15 minutes drive from Luton, Milton Keynes and Aylesbury. Follow the brown tourist signs in Leighton Buzzard or from the A505. Pages Park Station is ¾ mile from the Town Centre on the A4146 Hemel Hempstead road.

LLANBERIS LAKE RAILWAY

Address: Gilfach Ddu, Llanberis, Gwynedd LL55 4TY	**Nº of Steam Locos:** 3
Telephone Nº: (01286) 870549	**Nº of Other Locos:** 4
Year Formed: 1970	**Nº of Members:** –
Location of Line: Just off the A4086	**Annual Membership Fee:** –
Caernarfon to Capel Curig road at Llanberis	**Approx Nº of Visitors P.A.:** 70,000
Length of Line: 2 miles	**Gauge:** 1 foot 11½ inches

GENERAL INFORMATION

Nearest Railtrack Station: Bangor (8 miles)
Nearest Bus Station: Caernarfon (6 miles)
Car Parking: £1.20 Council car park on site
Coach Parking: Ample free parking on site
Souvenir Shop(s): Yes
Food & Drinks: Yes

SPECIAL INFORMATION

Llanberis Lake Railway runs along part of the trackbed of the Padarn Railway which transported slates for export and closed in 1961.

OPERATING INFORMATION

Opening Times: Open most days from March to October. Please send for a free timetable.
Steam Working: 11.00am to 4.00pm on most days.
Prices: Adult £4.10
Child £2.50

Detailed Directions by Car:
The railway is situated just off the A4086 Caernarfon to Capel Curig road. Follow signs for Padarn Country Park.

LLANGOLLEN RAILWAY

Address: The Station, Abbey Road, Llangollen, Denbighshire LL20 8SN
Telephone Nº: (01978) 860979
Year Formed: 1975
Location of Line: Valley of the River Dee from Llangollen to Carrog
Length of Line: 7½ miles

Nº of Steam Locos: 13
Nº of Other Locos: 9
Nº of Members: 1,500
Annual Membership Fee: Adult £12.00; Family £18.00
Approx Nº of Visitors P.A.: 90,000
Gauge: Standard

GENERAL INFORMATION

Nearest Railtrack Station: Ruabon (6 miles)
Nearest Bus Station: Wrexham (12 miles)
Car Parking: Public car park at Lower Dee Mill off A539 Ruabon road.
Coach Parking: Market Street car park in town centre
Souvenir Shop(s): Yes – at Llangollen Station
Food & Drinks: Yes – at Llangollen, Berwyn, Glyndyfrdwy and Carrog Stations.

SPECIAL INFORMATION

The route originally formed part of the line from Ruabon to Barmouth Junction, closed in 1964. The railway has been rebuilt by volunteers over the past 21 years, reopening to Carrog in 1996. The ultimate aim is to reopen to Corwen (10 miles).

OPERATING INFORMATION

Opening Times: Daily from May to October. Open weekends throughout the year. Opens from 10.00am to 6.00pm
Steam Working: Daily from 2nd May to 4th October and on various other days.
Prices: Adult Return £7.00 (Llangollen to Carrog)
Child Return £3.50
Family £17.50 (2 adults + 2 children)
Pensioners £5.20

Detailed Directions by Car:
From South & West: Go via the A5 to Llangollen. At the traffic lights turn into Castle Street to the River bridge; From North & East: Take the A483 to A539 junction and then via Trefor to Llangollen River bridge. The Station is adjacent to the River Dee.

LONGLEAT RAILWAY

Address: Longleat, near Warminster,
Wiltshire   BA12 7NW
Telephone Nº: (01985) 844579
Year Formed: 1970
Location of Line: Off A362 Frome to
Warminster road
Length of Line: 1¼ miles

Nº of Steam Locos: 1
Nº of Other Locos: 2
Nº of Members: –
Annual Membership Fee: –
Approx Nº of Visitors P.A.: Over 250,000
Gauge: 15 inches

GENERAL INFORMATION

Nearest Railtrack Station: Frome (3 miles),
Warminster (3½ miles)
Nearest Bus Station: Frome (3 miles), Warminster
(3½ miles)
Car Parking: 1,000 spaces available
Coach Parking: 250 spaces available
Souvenir Shop(s): Yes
Food & Drinks: Yes – 2 restaurants and a Cafe

SPECIAL INFORMATION

The line runs through parkland, woodland and,
after going through a tunnel, alongside a ½ mile
lake. From the train it is possible to view the wildlife
at the park including Sea Lions and many other
birds & animals. There are also a great number of
other attractions at the park.

OPERATING INFORMATION

Opening Times: Open from early March (15th) to
November (2nd). Also Santa Special trains on
Sundays from mid-November to December. Open
10.00am to 6.00pm.
Steam Working: Some Sundays and Santa Trains
Prices: Adult £1.50
        Child £1.50
        Family discount tickets are available

Detailed Directions by Car:
Longleat is situated 20 miles South of Bath, just off the A362 between Warminster and Frome.

Mangapps Railway Museum

Address: Southminster Road, Burnham-on-Crouch, Essex CM0 8QQ	**Nº of Steam Locos:** 3
Telephone Nº: (01621) 784898	**Nº of Other Locos:** 6
Year Formed: 1989	**Nº of Members:** –
Location of Line: Mangapps Farm	**Annual Membership Fee:** –
Length of Line: ¾ mile	**Approx Nº of Visitors P.A.:** 20,000
	Gauge: Standard

GENERAL INFORMATION

Nearest Railtrack Station: Burnham-on-Crouch (1 mile)
Nearest Bus Station: –
Car Parking: Ample free parking at site
Coach Parking: Ample free parking at site
Souvenir Shop(s): Yes
Food & Drinks: Yes – drinks and snacks only

SPECIAL INFORMATION

The Railway endeavours to recreate the atmosphere of an East Anglian light railway. It also includes an extensive museum with an emphasis on East Anglian items and signalling.

OPERATING INFORMATION

Opening Times: Closed during January and February. Then open every weekend and bank holiday (except over Christmas). Open daily during the School summer holidays.
Steam Working: 1st Sunday of the month and bank holidays. Diesel at other times.
Prices: Adult – Steam £4.00; Diesel £3.50
        Child – Steam £2.50; Diesel £2.00
The Museum sometimes has special events running. Please phone for details.

Detailed Directions by Car:
From South & West: From M25 take either the A12 or A127 and then the A130 to Rettendon Turnpike and then follow signs to Burnham; From North: From A12 take A414 to Oak Corner then follow signs to Burnham.

THE MIDDLETON RAILWAY

Address: The Station, Moor Road, Hunslet, Leeds   LS10 2JQ
Telephone Nº: (0113) 271-0320
Web Site: http://www.bmcl.demon.co.uk/mrt/
Year Formed: 1960
Location of Line: Moor Road to Middleton Park

Length of Line: 1½ miles
Nº of Steam Locos: 15
Nº of Other Locos: 12
Annual Membership Fee: Adults £8.00
Approx Nº of Visitors P.A.: 32,200
Gauge: Standard

GENERAL INFORMATION

Nearest Railtrack Station: Leeds City (1 mile)
Nearest Bus Station: Leeds (1½ miles)
Car Parking: Free parking at site
Coach Parking: Free parking at site
Souvenir Shop(s): Yes
Food & Drinks: Yes

SPECIAL INFORMATION

The Middleton Railway is a direct descendant of Branding's Railway (1758) and was the first site to successfully use steam locos in 1812. It was also the first standard gauge railway to be taken over by a preservation society in 1960.

OPERATING INFORMATION

Opening Times: Weekends & Bank Holidays from Easter to 1st January. Open 9.30am to 5.00pm
Steam Working: 10.30am to 5.00pm on operating days.
Prices: Adult £2.00
            Child £1.00
            Family £5.00 (2 adults + 2 children)
Tickets provide for unlimited travel on the day of issue.
Please telephone for the timetable and details of special events.

Detailed Directions by Car:
From All Parts: Exit the M1 at junction 45, turn right at the top of the slip road and take 3rd exit at the roundabout. The entrance to the Railway is 50 yards on the right. The railway is also signposted from the A61 and A653.

MID-HANTS RAILWAY

Address: The Railway Station, Alresford, Hampshire SO24 9JG **Telephone No:** (01962) 733810 General enquiries; (01962) 734866 Timetable **Year Formed:** 1977 **Location of Line:** Alresford to Alton **Length of Line:** 10 miles	**No of Steam Locos:** 19 **No of Other Locos:** 4 **No of Members:** 4,000 **Annual Membership Fee:** Adult £10.00 **Approx No of Visitors P.A.:** 120,000 **Gauge:** Standard

GENERAL INFORMATION

Nearest Railtrack Station: Alton (adjacent) or Winchester (7 miles)
Nearest Bus Station: Winchester (7 miles)
Car Parking: Pay and display at Alton and Alresford Stations (Alresford free on Sundays & Bank Holidays)
Coach Parking: By arrangement at Alresford Station
Souvenir Shop(s): At Alresford, Ropley & Alton
Food & Drinks: Yes – Buffet on most trains. 'West Country' buffet at Alresford

SPECIAL INFORMATION

The railway runs through four fully restored stations and has a Loco yard and picnic area at Ropley.

OPERATING INFORMATION

Opening Times: Weekends & Bank Holidays from March to October. Daily for most of June, July and August and for most School Holidays. Weekends and other dates in December.
Steam Working: All operating days.
Prices: Adult £7.50
　　　　　Child (age 5 to 15) £4.50
　　　　　Senior Citizens £5.50
　　　　　Family £22.00 (2 adults + 4 children)
A 15% discount off these prices is available for pre-booked parties of 15 or more people. Write or call for a booking form.

Detailed Directions by Car:
From the East: Take M25 then A3 and A31 to Alton; From the North: Take M1 then M25 and M3 to Winchester. Then take A31 to Alton.

MIDLAND RAILWAY CENTRE

Address: Butterley Station, Ripley, Derbyshire DE5 3QZ	**Nº of Steam Locos**: 26
Telephone Nº: (01773) 747674	**Nº of Other Locos**: 48
Year Formed: 1969	**Nº of Members**: 2,000
Location of Line: Butterley, near Ripley	**Annual Membership Fee**: £12.00
Length of Line: Standard gauge 3½ miles, Narrow gauge 0.8 mile	**Approx Nº of Visitors P.A.**: 130,000
	Gauge: Standard and various Narrow gauges

GENERAL INFORMATION

Nearest Railtrack Station: Alfreton (6 miles)
Nearest Bus Station: Bus stop outside Butterley Station.
Car Parking: Free parking at site – ample space
Coach Parking: Free parking at site
Souvenir Shop(s): Yes – at Butterley and Swanwick
Food & Drinks: Yes – both sites + bar on train

SPECIAL INFORMATION

The Centre is a unique project with a huge Museum development together with narrow gauge, miniature & model railways as well as a country park and farm park.

OPERATING INFORMATION

Opening Times: The centre is open almost daily – trains do not run every day it is open however.
Steam Working: Trains run most weekends and bank holidays throughout the year. Trains also run during most days in the school holidays. Phone for further timetable details.
Prices: Adult £7.95
          Child £1.00
          Senior Citizens £6.50

Detailed Directions by Car:
From All Parts: From the M1 exit at Junction 28 and take the A38 towards Derby. The Centre is signposted at the junction with the B6179.

MOORS VALLEY RAILWAY

Address: Moors Valley Country Park, Horton Road, Ashley Heath, Nr. Ringwood, Hants. BH24 2ET Telephone N°: (01425) 471415 Year Formed: 1985 Location of Line: Moors Valley Country Park	Length of Line: 1 mile N° of Steam Locos: 13 N° of Other Locos: – N° of Members: – Annual Membership Fee: – Approx N° of Visitors P.A.: – Gauge: 7¼ inches

GENERAL INFORMATION

Nearest Railtrack Station: Bournemouth (12 miles)
Nearest Bus Station: Ringwood (3 miles)
Car Parking: Parking charge varies throughout the year. Maximum charge £3.50 per day.
Coach Parking: Charges are applied for parking
Souvenir Shop(s): Yes + Model Railway Shop
Food & Drinks: Yes

SPECIAL INFORMATION

The Moors Valley Railway is a complete small Railway with signalling and 2 signal boxes and also 4 tunnels and 2 level crossings.

OPERATING INFORMATION

Opening Times: Weekends from March to October. Sundays only from November to February. Daily from one week before to one week after Easter, Spring Bank Holiday to mid-September, during School half-term holidays and also from Boxing Day to end of School holidays.
Steam Working: 10.45am to 5.00pm when open.
Prices: Adult Return £2.00; Adult Single £1.05
    Child Return £1.35; Child Single 75p
Special party rates are available for 10 or more persons.

Detailed Directions by Car:
From All Parts: Moors Valley Country Park is situated on Horton Road which is off the A31 Ferndown to Ringwood road near the junction with the A338 to Bournemouth.

MULL & WEST HIGHLAND RAILWAY

Address: Old Pier Station, Craignure, Isle of Mull, Argyll   PA65 6AY
Telephone Nº: (01680) 812494
Web Site: http://www.zynet.co.uk/mull/rail
Year Formed: 1983
Location of Line: Isle of Mull
Length of Line: 1¼ miles

Gauge: 10¼ inches
Nº of Steam Locos: 3
Nº of Other Locos: 2 (3 later in Season)
Nº of Members: 30 (also Friends of the Railway)
Annual Membership Fee: £5.00
Approx Nº of Visitors P.A.: 30,000

GENERAL INFORMATION

Nearest Railtrack Station: Oban (11 miles by Cal-Mac Ferry)
Nearest Bus Station: Oban (as above)
Car Parking: Free parking on site at Craignure
Coach Parking: Free parking at site
Souvenir Shop(s): Yes
Food & Drinks: No – but drinks & sweets available

SPECIAL INFORMATION

This narrow gauge railway was the first railway to be built on a Scottish island. It was built specially to link Torosay Castle & Gardens to the main Port of entry.

OPERATING INFORMATION

Opening Times: Daily from April 9th to October 17th. Opens 11.00am to 5.00pm.
Steam Working: Steam and diesel trains are run depending on operational requirements.
Prices: Adult Single £2.00; Adult Return £3.00
Child Single £1.30; Child Return £2.00
Family Tickets (2 adults + 2 children)
Single £5.50; Return £7.50
Joint Sail/Rail tickets available from Cal-Mac in Oban.

Detailed Directions by Car:
Once off the ferry, turn left at the end of the pier, go straight on for almost ½ mile then turn left at the thistle sign opposite the Police station and carry straight on until you reach the station car park.

NENE VALLEY RAILWAY

Address: Wansford Station, Stibbington, Peterborough PE8 6LR	**N⁰ of Steam Locos:** 17
Telephone N⁰: (01780) 784444 enquiries; (01780) 784440 talking timetable & fax	**N⁰ of Other Locos:** 11
Year Formed: 1977	**N⁰ of Members:** 1,200
Location of Line: West of Peterborough	**Annual Membership Fee:** Adult £11.00; Child £6.00; Joint £17.50; OAP £6.00
Length of Line: 7½ miles	**Approx N⁰ of Visitors P.A.:** 60,000
	Gauge: Standard

GENERAL INFORMATION

Nearest Railtrack Station: Peterborough (¾ mile)
Nearest Bus Station: Peterborough (Queensgate – ¾ mile)
Car Parking: Free parking at Wansford, Ortonmere & Peterborough
Coach Parking: Free coach parking at Wansford
Souvenir Shop(s): Yes
Food & Drinks: Yes

SPECIAL INFORMATION

The railway is truly international in flavour with both British and Continental locomotives and rolling stock.

OPERATING INFORMATION

Opening Times: Sundays from mid-February to the end of October. Saturdays from Easter to end of October. Mid-week on various dates from May to the end of August. Open 10.00am to 5.50pm.
Steam Working: Most services are steam hauled apart from on diesel days and times of high fire risk.
Prices: Adult £7.50
            Child £3.50
            Family £17.50 (2 adults + 3 children)
            Senior Citizens/Disabled £6.00

Detailed Directions by Car:
The railway is situated off the southbound carriageway of the A1 between the A47 and A605 junctions – west of Peterborough and south of Stamford.

NORTHAMPTON & LAMPORT RAILWAY

Address: Pitsford & Bramford Station, Pitsford Road, Chapel Brampton, Northampton NN6 8BA **Telephone Nº:** (01604) 820327 (infoline) **Year Formed:** 1983 (became operational in November 1995) **Web Site:** http://www.nlr.org.uk	**Length of Line:** ¾ mile at present **Nº of Steam Locos:** 4 **Nº of Other Locos:** 8 **Nº of Members:** 600 **Annual Membership Fee:** £10.00 **Approx Nº of Visitors P.A.:** 22,000 **Gauge:** Standard

GENERAL INFORMATION

Nearest Railtrack Station: Northampton (5 miles)
Nearest Bus Station: Northampton (5 miles)
Car Parking: Free parking at site
Coach Parking: Free parking at site
Souvenir Shop(s): Yes
Food & Drinks: Yes

SPECIAL INFORMATION

A developing railway – this became operational again on 18th November 1995.

OPERATING INFORMATION

Opening Times: Most weekends and Bank holidays March to November. Santa Specials in December. Open 10.30am to 5.30pm
Steam Working: Diesel on Saturdays, Steam on Sundays.
Prices: Adult £2.60
Child £1.70
Family £7.20

Detailed Directions by Car:
The station is situated along the Pitsford road at Chapel Brampton, approximately 5 miles north of Northampton. Heading north out of town, it is signposted to the right on the A5199 (A50) Welford Road at Chapel Brampton crossroads or on the left on the A508 Market Harborough road at the Pitsford turn.

NORTH NORFOLK RAILWAY

Address: Sheringham Station, Sheringham, Norfolk NR26 8RA	**Nº of Steam Locos:** 6
Telephone Nº: (01623) 822045	**Nº of Other Locos:** 7
Year Formed: 1975	**Nº of Members:** 1,000
Location of Line: Sheringham to Holt via Weybourne	**Annual Membership Fee:** £12.00
Length of Line: 5¼ miles	**Approx Nº of Visitors P.A.:** 95,000
	Gauge: Standard

GENERAL INFORMATION

Nearest Railtrack Station: Sheringham (200 yards)
Nearest Bus Station: Outside the Station
Car Parking: Adjacent to all three stations
Coach Parking: Adjacent to all three stations
Souvenir Shop(s): Yes – at all three stations
Food & Drinks: Yes – main catering facilities at Sheringham Station

SPECIAL INFORMATION

Sheringham Station has a museum coach and signalbox. The railway is the only full-sized preserved railway in Norfolk.

OPERATING INFORMATION

Opening Times: February to December 9.30am to 5.30pm
Steam Working: 10.15am to 5.00pm
Prices: Adult £6.50
Child £3.50
Family £17.50
Senior Citizens £5.50
All the above prices are a return fare from Sheringham to Holt Stations.

Detailed Directions by Car:
The railway is situated on the A148 Holt to Cromer road. All 3 stations are signposted from this road.

NORTH YORKSHIRE MOORS RAILWAY

Address: Pickering Station, Pickering, North Yorkshire YO18 7AJ	**Nº of Steam Locos**: 20
Telephone Nº: (01751) 472508 (enquiries)	**Nº of Other Locos**: 12
Web Site: http://www.nymr.demon.co.uk/	**Nº of Members**: 8,000
Year Formed: 1967	**Annual Membership Fee**: Adult £12.00; Family £24.00
Location of Line: Pickering to Grosmont via stations at Levisham and Goathland	**Approx Nº of Visitors P.A.**: 280,000
Length of Line: 18 miles	**Gauge**: Standard

GENERAL INFORMATION

Nearest Railtrack Station: Grosmont (opposite NYMR station)
Nearest Bus Station: Pickering (½ mile)
Car Parking: Available at each station
Coach Parking: Available at Pickering & Grosmont
Souvenir Shop(s): Yes – at Pickering, Goathland and Grosmont
Food & Drinks: Yes – at Pickering and Grosmont

SPECIAL INFORMATION

The NYMR runs through the spectacular North Yorks Moors and is the most popular in the country. As seen in 'Heartbeat'.

OPERATING INFORMATION

Opening Times: Open daily from March 21st to November 1st
Steam Working: Daily – please phone for timetable information
Prices: Adult £8.90
Child £4.50
Family Tickets start at £20.90 for 2 adults & 1 child – ring for further details.

Detailed Directions by Car:
From the South: Follow signs to York, follow the A64 to Malton then take the A169 from Malton to Pickering; From the North: Take A171 to Whitby and then the A169 to Grosmont.

NOTTINGHAM HERITAGE CENTRE

Address: Nottingham Heritage Centre, Mere Way, Ruddington, Nottingham NG11 6NX
Telephone Nº: (0115) 940-5705
Fax Nº: (0115) 940-5905
Year Formed: 1990 (Opened in 1994)
Location of Line: Ruddington to

Loughborough Junction
Length of Line: 1 mile at present
Nº of Steam Locos: 7
Nº of Other Locos: 7
Nº of Members: 49
Annual Membership Fee: £8.00
Approx Nº of Visitors P.A.: 9,000

GENERAL INFORMATION

Nearest Railtrack Station: Nottingham (5 miles)
Nearest Bus Station: Bus service from Nottingham to the Centre
Car Parking: Free parking at site
Coach Parking: Free parking at site
Souvenir Shop(s): Yes
Food & Drinks: Yes

SPECIAL INFORMATION

The Heritage Centre covers an area of over eleven acres and is set within the Rushcliffe Country Park in Ruddington. A further 2.7 miles of line is currently undergoing restoration.

OPERATING INFORMATION

Opening Times: Every Sunday and Bank Holiday from Easter Sunday to 18th October. Open 10.45am to 5.30pm
Steam Working: Steam train service every 30 minutes from 11.00am to 5.00pm
Prices: Adult £2.50 (£3.00 Bank Holidays & Special Events)
Child £1.50
Senior Citizens £2.00 or £2.50
Family £7 or £8 (2 adults + 3 children)

Detailed Directions by Car:
From All Parts: The centre is situated off the A60 Nottingham to Loughborough Road and is signposted just south of the traffic lights at Ruddington.

PAIGNTON & DARTMOUTH STEAM RAILWAY

Address: Queen's Park Station, Torbay Road, Paignton   TQ4 6AF
Telephone Nº: (01803) 555872
Year Formed: 1973
Location of Line: Paignton to Kingswear
Length of Line: 7 miles

Nº of Steam Locos: 5
Nº of Other Locos: 3
Nº of Members: 250
Annual Membership Fee: Adult £10.00; Senior Citizens £8.00; Children £6.00
Approx Nº of Visitors P.A.: 350,000
Gauge: Standard

GENERAL INFORMATION

Nearest Railtrack Station: Paignton (adjacent)
Nearest Bus Station: Paignton (2 minutes walk)
Car Parking: Multi-storey or Railtrack car park
Coach Parking: Multi-storey (3 minutes walk)
Souvenir Shop(s): Yes – at Paignton & Kingswear
Food & Drinks: Yes – at Paignton & Kinswear

SPECIAL INFORMATION

A passenger ferry is available from Kingswear Station across to Dartmouth. A number of combined excursions are available including train and river trips.

OPERATING INFORMATION

Opening Times: Open daily from June to September (inclusive). Also open days in April, May, October and December (phone for details).
Steam Working: Trains run throughout the day from 10.15am to 5.00pm
Prices: Adult Return £6.10
Child Return £4.10
Family Return £18.50 (2 adults + 2 children)

Detailed Directions by Car:
From All Parts: Take the M5 to Exeter and then the A380 to Paignton.

PEAK RAIL PLC

Address: Matlock Station, Matlock, Derbyshire DE4 3NA	**Nº of Steam Locos:** 2
Telephone Nº: (01629) 580381	**Nº of Other Locos:** 9
Year Formed: 1975	**Nº of Members:** 1,500
Location of Line: Matlock Riverside to Rowsley South	**Annual Membership Fee:** Adult £12.00
Length of Line: 4½ miles	**Approx Nº of Visitors P.A.:** 10,000+
	Gauge: Standard

GENERAL INFORMATION

Nearest Railtrack Station: Matlock (500 yards)
Nearest Bus Station: Matlock
Car Parking: Paid car parking at Matlock Station, 200 spaces at Rowsley South Station, 20 spaces at Darley Dale Station
Coach Parking: Free parking at Rowsley South
Souvenir Shop(s): Yes
Food & Drinks: Yes

SPECIAL INFORMATION

The Palatine Restaurant Car is available whilst travelling on the train and caters for Sunday Lunches, Saturday Evening Meals and Party Bookings. Coach parties are welcomed for afternoon teas when the railway is operating.

OPERATING INFORMATION

Opening Times: Sundays in January, February, March and November. Weekends during the rest of the year. Wednesdays in June and July. Every day but Mondays and Fridays in August. Also other dates.
Steam Working: All services throughout the year.
Prices: Adult Return £5.00; Adult Single £2.50
Senior Citizen Return £3.50; Single £1.75
Children up to the age of 12 travel free
Children 12 to 15 £2.50

Detailed Directions by Car:
Exit the M1 at Junctions 28, 29 or 30 and follow signs towards Matlock. From North and South take A6 direct to Matlock. From Stoke-on-Trent, take the A52 to Ashbourne, then the A5035 to Matlock. Upon reaching Matlock follow the brown tourist signs.

RAVENGLASS & ESKDALE RAILWAY

Address: Ravenglass, Cumbria
CA18 1SW
Telephone Nº: (01229) 717171
Year Formed: 1876
Location of Line: Ravenglass
Length of Line: 7 miles
Gauge: 15 inches

Nº of Steam Locos: 6
Nº of Other Locos: 7
Nº of Members: 2,100
Annual Membership Fee: Adult £10.00;
Children £5.00
Approx Nº of Visitors P.A.: 250,000

GENERAL INFORMATION

Nearest Railtrack Station: Ravenglass (adjacent)
Nearest Bus Station: No bus service
Car Parking: Available at both terminals
Coach Parking: At Ravenglass
Souvenir Shop(s): Yes
Food & Drinks: Yes

SPECIAL INFORMATION

This railway travels from the Cumbria coast into England's highest hills and is England's oldest narrow-gauge railway.

OPERATING INFO

Opening Times: The service runs daily from the beginning of March until the end of November. Also runs during selected weekends in the Winter. Open from 8.00am to 5.00pm
Steam Working: Most services are steam hauled.
Prices: Adult £6.30
Child £3.30
Senior Citizens £5.80
Family £14.90

Detailed Directions by Car:
The railway is situated on the A595 Barrow to Whitehaven road. Follow signs for the turn-off to Ravenglass.

ROMNEY, HYTHE & DYMCHURCH RAILWAY

Address: New Romney Station, New Romney, Kent TN28 8PL **Telephone Nº:** (01797) 362353 **Year Formed:** 1927 **Location of Line:** Approximately 4 miles south of Folkestone **Length of Line:** 13½ miles	**Nº of Steam Locos:** 11 **Nº of Other Locos:** 5 **Nº of Members:** – **Annual Membership Fee:** Supporters association – Adult £12.00; Junior £7.50 **Approx Nº of Visitors P.A.:** 150,000 **Gauge:** 15 inches

GENERAL INFORMATION

Nearest Railtrack Station: Folkestone Central (4 miles)
Nearest Bus Station: Folkestone (then take bus to Hythe)
Car Parking: Available at all major stations
Coach Parking: At New Romney & Dungeness
Souvenir Shop(s): Yes – 4 at various stations
Food & Drinks: 2 Cafes serving food and drinks

SPECIAL INFORMATION

Opened in 1927 as 'The World's Smallest Public Railway'. Now the only 15" gauge tourist main line railway in the world. Double track, 6 stations.

OPERATING INFORMATION

Opening Times: A daily service runs from Easter to the last Sunday in September. Open at weekends in March and October and for Santa Specials in December.
Steam Working: All operational days.
Prices: Depend on length of journey. Maximums:
    Adult £8.60
    Child £4.30
    Family £28.60 (2 adult + 3 children)
Family tickets are only available from New Romney Station.

Detailed Directions by Car:
Exit the M20 at Junction 11 then follow signs to Hythe and the brown tourist signs for the railway. Alternatively, Take the A259 to New Romney and follow the brown tourist signs for the railway.

SEVERN VALLEY RAILWAY

Address: Railway Station, Bewdley, Worcs. DY12 1BG
Telephone Nº: (01299) 403816
Year Formed: 1965
Location of Line: Kidderminster (Worcs.) to Bridgnorth (Shropshire)
Length of Line: 16 miles

Nº of Steam Locos: 27
Nº of Other Locos: 12
Nº of Members: 15,000
Annual Membership Fee: Adult £10.00
Approx Nº of Passengers P.A.: 203,000
Gauge: Standard

GENERAL INFORMATION

Nearest Railtrack Station: Kidderminster (adjacent)
Nearest Bus Station: Kidderminster (500 yards)
Car Parking: Large car park at Kidderminster. Spaces also available at other stations.
Coach Parking: Available at Kidderminster
Souvenir Shop(s): At Kidderminster & Bridgnorth
Food & Drinks: Yes – on most trains. Also at Kidderminster, Bewdley and Bridgnorth

SPECIAL INFORMATION

The SVR has numerous special events including a Spring and Autumn Steam Gala, 1940's weekend, Heavy horse weekend and visits by Thomas the Tank Engine and Santa!

OPERATING INFORMATION

Opening Times: Weekends throughout the year. Also daily from May 23rd to the October 11th and School holidays.
Steam Working: Train times vary depending on timetable information. Phone for details.
Prices: Vary depending on journey taken: Family Day Rover £20.00 (2 adults + 2 children)

Detailed Directions by Car:
For Kidderminster take M5 and exit Junction 3 or Junction 6. Follow the brown tourist signs for the railway; From the South: Take the M40 then M42 to Junction 1 for the A448 from Bromsgrove to Kidderminster.

SITTINGBOURNE & KEMSLEY LIGHT RAILWAY

Address: The Wall, Milton Regis, Sittingbourne, Kent ME7 4QG	**N⁰ of Steam Locos:** 8
Telephone N⁰: (01795) 424899	**N⁰ of Other Locos:** 3
Year Formed: 1969	**N⁰ of Members:** 200
Location of Line: North of Sittingbourne	**Annual Membership Fee:** £10.00
Length of Line: 2 miles	**Approx N⁰ of Visitors P.A.:** 5,000
	Gauge: 2 feet 6 inches

GENERAL INFORMATION

Nearest Railtrack Station: Sittingbourne (¼ mile)
Nearest Bus Station: Sittingbourne Railtrack station
Car Parking: Available in Sittingbourne
Coach Parking: Available in Sittingbourne
Souvenir Shop(s): Yes
Food & Drinks: Yes

SPECIAL INFORMATION

The railway runs on a narrow gauge line which originally was a paper company industrial system.

OPERATING INFORMATION

Opening Times: Easter to September, Sundays and Bank Holiday Mondays. Also Wednesdays and Saturdays in August.
Steam Working: Trains run from 1.30pm normally, but from 11.30am on Bank Holidays & School Holidays.
Prices: Adult £2.60
Child £1.30
Senior Citizens £1.80
Family £7.00

Detailed Directions by Car:
From East or West: Take the M2 (or M20) to A249 and travel towards Sittingbourne. Turn onto the A2 for Sittingbourne, carry on until the traffic lights, turn left into Chalkwell Road. ¼ mile to a roundabout, take the right hand exit. Go 400 yards to Mill Way roundabout, turn right and 300 yards on the left is the car park.

SNOWDON MOUNTAIN RAILWAY

Address: Llanberis, Caernarfon, Gwynedd, Wales LL55 4TY	**Length of Line:** 4¾ miles
Telephone Nº: (01286) 870223	**Nº of Steam Locos:** 7 (only 5 operating)
Fax Nº: (01286) 872518	**Nº of Other Locos:** 4 + 3 Railcars
Year Formed: 1894	**Nº of Members:** –
Location of Line: Llanberis to Snowdon summit	**Annual Membership Fee:** –
	Approx Nº of Visitors P.A.: 150,000
	Gauge: 2 feet 7½ inches

GENERAL INFORMATION

Nearest Railtrack Station: Bangor (8½ miles)
Nearest Bus Station: Caernarfon (7½ miles)
Car Parking: Llanberis Station car park – £1.00
Also other car parks nearby
Coach Parking: As above but space is very limited at busy times.
Souvenir Shop(s): Yes
Food & Drinks: Yes

SPECIAL INFORMATION

Britain's only public rack and pinion mountain railway. Climbs over 3,000 feet to Snowdon summit. Round trip approximately 2½ hours.

OPERATING INFORMATION

Opening Times: Open daily (weather permitting) from 15th March to 1st November. Trains run from 9.00am (8.30pm in Peak season) until late afternoon. Subject to passenger demand.
Steam Working: Normally at least one steam loco on passenger service, but not guaranteed early or late in the season.
Prices: Adult £14.80
 Child £10.70
 Family £40.00 (2 adults + 2 children)
Family tickets only available early morning.
Special rates for groups of 15 or more people.

Detailed Directions by Car:
Llanberis Station is situated on the A4086 Caernarfon to Capel Curig road, 7½ miles from Caernarfon. Convenient access via the main North Wales coast road (A55). Exit at the A55/A5 junction and follow signs to Llanberis via B4366, B4547 and A4086.

SOUTH DEVON RAILWAY

Address: Buckfastleigh Station, Buckfastleigh, Devon TQ11 0DZ	**N° of Steam Locos:** 16
Telephone N°: (01364) 642338	**N° of Other Locos:** 7
Year Formed: 1969	**N° of Members:** 1,300
Location of Line: Totnes to Buckfastleigh via Staverton	**Annual Membership Fee:** £8.00
	Approx N° of Visitors P.A.: 80,000
Length of Line: 7 miles	**Gauge:** Standard

GENERAL INFORMATION

Nearest Railtrack Station: Totnes (¼ mile)
Nearest Bus Station: Totnes (½ mile), Buckfastleigh (Station Road)
Car Parking: Free parking at Buckfastleigh, Council/BR parking at Totnes
Coach Parking: As above
Souvenir Shop(s): Yes – Buckfastleigh & on train
Food & Drinks: Yes – at Buckfastleigh & on train

SPECIAL INFORMATION

The railway was opened in 1872 as the Totnes, Buckfastleigh & Ashburton Railway.

OPERATING INFORMATION

Opening Times: Tuesdays, Wednesdays, Saturdays and Sundays in April and May. Daily during the Easter Holidays and from May 16th to October 4th. Also open during October half-term and on Tuesdays, Saturdays and Sundays in October.
Steam Working: Almost all trains are steam hauled
Prices: Adult £5.90
         Child £3.90
         Family £17.60

Detailed Directions by Car:
Buckfastleigh is half way between Exeter and Plymouth on the A38 Devon Expressway. Totnes can be reached by taking the A385 from Paignton and Torquay. Brown tourist signs give directions for the railway.

SOUTH TYNEDALE RAILWAY

Address: The Railway Station, Alston, Cumbria   CA9 3JB
Telephone Nº: (01434) 381696 (Enquiries) (01434) 382828 (Talking timetable)
Year Formed: 1973
Location of Line: From Alston, northwards along South Tyne Valley.

Length of Line: 2 miles
Nº of Steam Locos: 5
Nº of Other Locos: 6
Nº of Members: 300
Annual Membership Fee: £8.00
Approx Nº of Visitors P.A.: 25,000
Gauge: 2 feet

GENERAL INFORMATION

Nearest Railtrack Station: Haltwhistle (15 miles)
Nearest Bus Station: At Alston Station during Summer months.
Car Parking: Free parking at Alston Station
Coach Parking: Free parking at Alston Station
Souvenir Shop(s): Yes
Food & Drinks: Yes

SPECIAL INFORMATION

The Society hopes to open the extension to Kirkhaugh in Northumberland (¾ mile) in 1998.

OPERATING INFO

Opening Times: Weekends from the beginning to April to the end of October. Open Thursdays in June and September then daily from 1st July to 6th September. Also open School half-terms in May and October and Santa Specials in December.
Steam Working: Varies, but generally weekends & Bank Holidays throughout the Summer & December weekends. Also daily from July 25th to August 31st.
Prices: Adult Return £2.50; Single £1.50
         Child Return £1.00; Single 75p
When the extension to Kirkhaugh opens, full fares will be more expensive due to the longer journey.

Detailed Directions by Car:
Alston can be reached by a number of roads from various directions including A689, A686 and the B6277. Alston Station is situated just off the A686 Hexham road, north of Alston Town Centre. Look for the brown tourist signs on roads into Alston.

SPA VALLEY RAILWAY

Address: West Station, Tunbridge Wells, Kent TN4 8NL	**N⁰ of Steam Locos:** 5
Telephone N⁰: (01892) 537715	**N⁰ of Other Locos:** 7
Year Formed: 1985	**N⁰ of Members:** Approximately 660
Location of Line: Tunbridge Wells West to Eridge (currently to Groombridge)	**Annual Membership Fee:** £10.00
Length of Line: 3½ miles operational	**Approx N⁰ of Visitors P.A.:** 18,000

GENERAL INFORMATION

Nearest Railtrack Station: Tunbridge Wells Central (½ mile)
Nearest Bus Stop: Outside Sainsbury's (100yds)
Car Parking: Available nearby
Coach Parking: Coach station in Montacute Road (150 yards)
Souvenir Shop(s): Yes
Food & Drinks: Yes

SPECIAL INFORMATION

The Railway's Tunbridge Wells Terminus is in a historic and unique L.B. & S.C.R. engine shed. The Railway's aims are to extend to Eridge to connect with the Main Line.

OPERATING INFORMATION

Opening Times: Weekends from April to October and also in December. Open most of July and August although closed on Mondays and Tuesdays. Also open various other dates.
Steam Working: Most services are steam-hauled. Trains run from 10.45am to 4.15pm.
Prices: Adult Return £3.50
              Child/Senior Citizen Return £2.00
              Unlimited Day Travel £5.00
Parties of 20 or more will be charged £2.00 per head.

Detailed Directions by Car:
The Spa Valley Railway is in the southern part of Tunbridge Wells, a 100 yards off the A26. Station is adjacent to Sainsbury's and Homebase. Car Parks are nearby in Major Yorks Road, Union House & Linden Close.

STRATHSPEY STEAM RAILWAY

Address: Aviemore Station, Dalfaber Road, Aviemore, Inverness-shire, PH22 1PY
Telephone Nº: (01479) 810725
Year Formed: 1971
Location of Line: Aviemore to Boat of Garten, Inverness-shire

Length of Line: 5 miles at present
Gauge: Standard
Nº of Steam Locos: 9
Nº of Other Locos: 6
Nº of Members: 800
Annual Membership Fee: £14.00
Approx Nº of Visitors P.A.: 45,000

GENERAL INFORMATION

Nearest Railtrack Station: Aviemore (600 yards)
Nearest Bus Station: Aviemore (600 yds)
Car Parking: Available at both stations
Coach Parking: At both stations
Souvenir Shop(s): Yes – both stations
Food & Drinks: Available on Steam trains only

SPECIAL INFORMATION

During 1998 the Railway will close Aviemore (Speyside) Station and move into Aviemore Station. This move is expected to take place in late May or early June. Please phone the Railway to confirm which station services are running from.

OPERATING INFO

Opening Times: Weekends and school holidays from the end of March to the end of October. Also Bank Holidays. Wednesdays and Thursdays in April, May & October. Daily from June to September & dates in December. Open 9.30am to 4.30pm.
Steam Working: Most trains are steam-hauled but diesel power is used whenever necessary.
Prices: Adult Return £5.00
             Child Return £2.50
             Family Return £12.50
             (2 adults + up to 3 children)

Detailed Directions by Car:
For Aviemore Station from South: Take the A9 then B970 and turn left between the railway & river bridges. For Boat of Garten from North; Take the A9 then A938 to Carr Bridge, then B9153 and A95 and follow the signs; From North East: Take A95 to Boat of Garten.

SWANAGE RAILWAY

Address: Station House, Railway Station, Swanage, Dorset BH19 1HB	**Nº of Steam Locos:** 5
Telephone Nº: (01929) 425800	**Nº of Other Locos:** 3
Year Formed: 1976	**Nº of Members:** 3,500
Location of Line: Swanage to Norden	**Annual Membership Fee:** Adult £13.00; Junior & Senior Citizens £8.00
Length of Line: 6 miles	**Approx Nº of Visitors P.A.:** 124,000
Gauge: Standard	

GENERAL INFORMATION

Nearest Railtrack Station: Wareham (10 miles)
Nearest Bus Station: Swanage Station (adjacent)
Car Parking: Park & Ride at Norden. Public car parks in Swanage (5 minutes walk)
Coach Parking: Available at Norden from mid-1997
Souvenir Shop(s): Yes – at Swanage Station
Food & Drinks: Yes – buffet available on trains and also Swanage Station Buffet.

SPECIAL INFORMATION

The railway runs along part of the route of the old Swanage to Wareham railway, opened in 1885.

OPERATING INFORMATION

Opening Times: Weekends throughout the year and daily from May to September. Opens from 9.30am to 5.00pm.
Steam Working: All services are steam-hauled
Prices: Adult £5.50
Child £2.75
Family £15.00

Detailed Directions by Car:
Norden Park & Ride Station is situated off the A351 on the approach to Corfe Castle. Swanage Station is situated in the centre of the town, just a few minutes walk from the beach. Take the A351 to reach Swanage.

TALYLLYN RAILWAY

Address: Wharf Station, Tywyn, Gwynedd, LL36 9EY
Telephone Nº: (01654) 710472
Year Formed: 1951
Location of Line: Tywyn to Nant Gwernol Station
Length of Line: 7¼ miles

Nº of Steam Locos: 6
Nº of Other Locos: 4
Nº of Members: 3,500
Annual Membership Fee: Adult £15.00
Approx Nº of Visitors P.A.: 53,000
Gauge: 2 feet 3 inches

GENERAL INFORMATION

Nearest Railtrack Station: Tywyn (300 yards)
Nearest Bus Station: Tywyn (300 yards)
Car Parking: 100 yards away
Coach Parking: Free parking (100 yards)
Souvenir Shop(s): Yes
Food & Drinks: Yes

SPECIAL INFORMATION

Talyllyn Railway was the first preserved railway in the world – saved from closure in 1951. The railway was opened in 1866 to carry slate from Bryn Eglwys Quarry to Tywyn.

OPERATING INFO

Opening Times: Daily from March 30th to October 31st. Generally open from 10.00am to mid or late afternoon.
Steam Working: All passenger trains are steam-hauled.
Prices: Adult Return £8.00
            Child Return £4.00
Children pay £2.00 if travelling with an adult. Otherwise, they pay half adult fare. The fares shown above are for a full round trip. Tickets to intermediate stations are cheaper.

Detailed Directions by Car:
From the North: Take the A493 from Dolgellau into Tywyn; From the South: Take the A493 from Machynlleth to Tywyn.

TANFIELD RAILWAY

Address: Marley Hill Engine Shed, Old Marley Hill, Gateshead, Tyne & Wear NE16 5ET	**Length of Line:** 3 miles
	Nº of Steam Locos: 25
Telephone Nº: (01207) 280643	**Nº of Other Locos:** 9
Year Formed: 1976	**Nº of Members:** 150
Location of Line: Between Sunniside & East Tanfield, Co. Durham	**Annual Membership Fee:** £7.00
	Approx Nº of Visitors P.A.: 25,000
	Gauge: Standard

GENERAL INFORMATION

Nearest Railtrack Station: Newcastle-upon-Tyne (8 miles)
Nearest Bus Station: Gateshead Interchange (6 miles)
Car Parking: Spaces for 100 cars
Coach Parking: Spaces for 6 or 7 coaches only
Souvenir Shop(s): Yes
Food & Drinks: Yes – light snacks only

SPECIAL INFORMATION

Tanfield Railway is the oldest existing railway in use – it was originally opened in 1725. It also runs beside the oldest railway bridge in the world, The Causey Arch.

OPERATING INFORMATION

Opening Times: Every Sunday & Bank Holiday Monday throughout the year. Also opens on Wednesdays & Thursdays in Summer school holidays.
Steam Working: Trains run 11.00am to 4.00pm (11.30am to 3.15pm in the Winter).
Prices: Adult £3.50
Child £2.00
Family £8.50 (2 adults + 2 children)

Detailed Directions by Car:
Sunniside Station is off the A6076 Sunniside to Stanley road in Co. Durham. To reach the Railway, leave A1(M) and follow signs for Beamish museum at Chester-le-Street then continue to Stanley and follow Tanfield Railway signs.

TEIFI VALLEY RAILWAY

Address: Henllan Station, Henllan, near Newcastle Emlyn, Carmarthenshire
Telephone Nº: (01559) 371077
Year Formed: 1972
Location of Line: Between Cardigan and Carmarthen off the A484
Length of Line: 2 miles

Nº of Steam Locos: 2
Nº of Other Locos: 3
Nº of Members: Approximately 150
Annual Membership Fee: £10.00
Approx Nº of Visitors P.A.: 40,000

GENERAL INFORMATION

Nearest Railtrack Station: Carmarthen (10 miles)
Nearest Bus Station: Carmarthen (10 miles)
Car Parking: Spaces for 70 cars available.
Coach Parking: Spaces for 4 coaches available.
Souvenir Shop(s): Yes
Food & Drinks: Yes

SPECIAL INFORMATION

The Railway was formerly part of the G.W.R. but now runs on a Narrow Gauge using Quarry Engines. A new 7¼ inch miniature will be running during 1998.

OPERATING INFORMATION

Opening Times: Open daily from Easter until the end of October. Also open on some days in December for 'Santa Specials'. Open 10.00am to 6.00pm.
Steam Working: Monday to Wednesday & Bank Holidays when open. Also on Thursdays during July, August and early September.
Prices: Adult £5.00
Child £3.00
Group discounts are available.

Detailed Directions by Car:
From All Parts: The Railway is situated off the A484 between Carmarthen and Cardigan. It is approximately 10 miles from Carmarthen and 15 miles from Cardigan.

TELFORD STEAM RAILWAY

Address: The Old Loco Shed, Bridge Road, Horsehay, Telford, Shropshire **Telephone Nº:** (01952) 503880 **Year Formed:** 1976 **Location of Line:** Based at Horsehay & Dawley Station	**Length of Line:** ½ mile standard gauge, an eighth of a mile 2 foot narrow gauge **Nº of Steam Locos:** 6 **Nº of Other Locos:** 7 **Nº of Members:** Approximately 150 **Annual Membership Fee:** – **Approx Nº of Visitors P.A.:** 10,000

GENERAL INFORMATION

Nearest Railtrack Station: Wellington or Telford Central
Nearest Bus Station: Dawley (1 mile)
Car Parking: Free parking at the site
Coach Parking: Free parking at the site
Souvenir Shop(s): Yes – 'Freight Stop Gift Shop'
Food & Drinks: Yes – 'Horsehay Company Café'

SPECIAL INFORMATION

Telford Steam Railway has both a Standard Gauge and Narrow Gauge line as well as Miniature and Model Railways.

OPERATING INFORMATION

Opening Times: Every Sunday and Bank Holiday between Easter and the end of September. Open 11.00am to 4.00pm except for Bank Holidays when it is open until 5.00pm
Steam Working: 2 foot gauge on all operating days. Standard gauge on the last Sunday of the month and also on Bank Holidays.
Prices: Adult all day tickets £2.50
         Child all day tickets £1.50

Detailed Directions by Car:
From All Parts: Exit the M54 at Junction 6 and take the A5223 to Ironbridge. At the third traffic island, turn left and the Railway is a further 400 yards on the left.

VALE OF RHEIDOL RAILWAY

Address: The Locomotive Shed, Park Avenue, Aberystwyth, Dyfed SY23 1PG	**Nº of Steam Locos:** 3
Telephone Nº: (01970) 625819	**Nº of Other Locos:** 1
Year Formed: 1902	**Nº of Members:** None
Location of Line: Aberystwyth to Devil's Bridge	**Annual Membership Fee:** –
Length of Line: 11¾ miles	**Approx Nº of Visitors P.A.:** 37,000
	Gauge: 1 foot 11¾ inches

GENERAL INFORMATION

Nearest Railtrack Station: Aberystwyth (adjacent)
Nearest Bus Station: Aberystwyth (adjacent)
Car Parking: 2 short stay + 2 long stay car parks within 400 yards.
Coach Parking: Parking available 400 yards away.
Souvenir Shop(s): Yes
Food & Drinks: Yes

SPECIAL INFORMATION

The journey between the stations take one hour in each direction. At Devil's Bridge there is a cafe, toilets, a picnic area and the famous Mynach Falls. The line climbs over 600 feet in 11¾ miles.

OPERATING INFORMATION

Opening Times: Open almost every day from 10th April to 29th October. Closed Mondays & Fridays in April & October. Closed some Fridays in May & September.
Steam Working: All trains are steam-hauled. Trains run from 10.30am to 4.00pm on most days.
Prices: Adult Return £10.50
Child Return – First 2 children per adult pay £1.00 each. Further children pay £5.25.

Detailed Directions by Car:
From the North take A487 into Aberystwyth. From the East take A470 and A44 to Aberystwyth. From the South take A487 or A485 to Aberystwyth. The Station is joined on to the Railtrack Station in Alexandra Road.

WELLS & WALSINGHAM LIGHT RAILWAY

Address: The Station, Wells-next-the-Sea, NR23 1QB
Telephone Nº: (01328) 710631
Year Formed: 1982
Location of Line: Wells-next-the-Sea to Walsingham, Norfolk
Length of Line: 4 miles

Nº of Steam Locos: 1
Nº of Other Locos: 1
Nº of Members: 50
Annual Membership Fee: £11.00
Approx Nº of Visitors P.A.: 20,000
Gauge: 10¼ inches

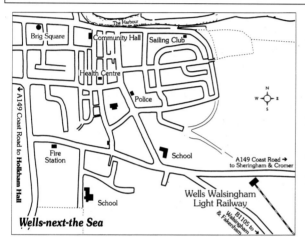

GENERAL INFORMATION

Nearest Railtrack Station: King's Lynn (21 miles)
Nearest Bus Station: Norwich (24 miles)
Car Parking: Free parking at site
Coach Parking: Free parking at site
Souvenir Shop(s): Yes
Food & Drinks: Yes

SPECIAL INFORMATION

The Railway is the longest narrow-gauge steam railway in the world. The course of the railway is famous for wildlife and butterflies in season.

OPERATING INFORMATION

Opening Times: Daily from Good Friday to the End of September.
Steam Working: Trains run from 10.15am on operating days.
Prices: Adult Return £5.00
Child Return £3.50

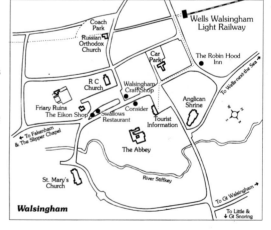

Detailed Directions by Car:
Wells-next-the-Sea is situated on the North Norfolk Coast midway between Hunstanton and Cromer. The Main Station is situated on the main A149 Stiffkey Road. Follow the brown tourist signs for the Railway.

WELSH HIGHLAND RAILWAY LTD.

Address: Gelert Farm Works, Madog Street West, Porthmadog, Gwynedd, LL49 9DY **Telephone Nº:** (01766) 513402 **Year Formed:** 1964 **Location of Line:** Tremadog Road, Porthmadog, Gwynedd LL49 9DY	**Length of Line:** ¾ mile **Nº of Steam Locos:** 7 **Nº of Other Locos:** 18 **Nº of Members:** 1,200 **Annual Membership Fee:** £10.00 Adult **Approx Nº of Visitors P.A.:** 20,000 **Gauge:** 60 centimetres

GENERAL INFORMATION

Nearest Railtrack Station: Porthmadog (50 yards)
Nearest Bus Station: Services 1 & 3 stop 200 yards away
Car Parking: Free parking at site, also 2 public car parks within 100 yards.
Coach Parking: Adjacent
Souvenir Shop(s): Yes – large range of books, videos and souvenirs.
Food & Drinks: Yes

SPECIAL INFORMATION

The West Highland Railway is a family-orientated attraction based around a Railway Heritage Centre.

OPERATING INFORMATION

Opening Times: Daily from 16th May to 27th September. Also open on Bank Holiday weeks, weekends in May and some weekends in October.
Steam Working: Most weekends and every day in August.
Prices: Adult Return £2.00
Child Return £1.25
Senior Citizen Return £1.75
Family Return £6.00
(2 adults + 2 children)
Children under 5 are admitted free of charge

Detailed Directions by Car:
From Bangor/Caernarfon take the A487 to Porthmadog. From Pwllheli take the A497 to Porthmadog then turn left at the roundabout. From the Midlands take A487 to Portmadog. Once in Porthmadog, follow the brown tourist signs. The line is located right next to Porthmadog Railtrack Station.

WELSHPOOL & LLANFAIR LIGHT RAILWAY

Address: The Station, Llanfair Caereinion, Powys SY21 0SF	**Nº of Steam Locos:** 6
Telephone Nº: (01938) 810441	**Nº of Other Locos:** 3
Year Formed: 1959	**Nº of Members:** 2,750
Location of Line: Welshpool to Llanfair Caereinion, Mid Wales	**Annual Membership Fee:** £12.50
Length of Line: 8 miles	**Approx Nº of Visitors P.A.:** 25,000
	Gauge: 2 feet 6 inches

GENERAL INFORMATION

Nearest Railtrack Station: Welshpool (1 mile)
Nearest Bus Station: Welshpool (1 mile)
Car Parking: Free parking at Welshpool and Llanfair Caereinion
Coach Parking: As above
Souvenir Shop(s): Yes – at both ends of line
Food & Drinks: Yes – at Llanfair only

SPECIAL INFORMATION

The railway has the steepest gradient of any British railway, reaching a summit of 603 feet.

OPERATING INFORMATION

Opening Times: Easter holidays and weekends in April, May and September. Daily from 18th July to September 6th. Most other days in June and July and dates in October and December. Generally open from 10.30am to 4.00pm although trains may run earlier and later in the Summer season.
Steam Working: All trains are steam-hauled
Prices: Adult £7.50
Senior Citizens £6.50
Children under the age of 5 are free of charges. The first child aged 5-15 per adult is charged £1.00. All other children are charged half-price fare of £3.75

Detailed Directions by Car:
Both stations are situated alongside the A458 Shrewsbury to Dolgellau road and are clearly signposted

WEST LANCASHIRE LIGHT RAILWAY

Address: Station Road, Hesketh Bank, Nr. Preston, Lancashire PR4 6SP
Telephone Nº: (01772) 815881
Year Formed: 1967
Location of Line: On former site of Alty's Brickworks, Hesketh Bank
Length of Line: ¼ mile

Nº of Steam Locos: 5
Nº of Other Locos: –
Nº of Members: Approximately 70
Annual Membership Fee: £10.00 Adult; £15.00 Family
Approx Nº of Visitors P.A.: 10,000

GENERAL INFORMATION

Nearest Railtrack Station: Rufford (4 miles)
Nearest Bus Station: Preston (7 miles)
Car Parking: Space for 50 cars at site
Coach Parking: Space for 3 coaches at site
Souvenir Shop(s): Yes
Food & Drinks: Only soft drinks & snacks

SPECIAL INFORMATION

The Railway is run by volunteers and there is a large collection of Industrial Narrow Gauge equipment.

OPERATING INFO

Opening Times: Sundays and Bank Holidays throughout the year. No trains run from November to Easter (except Santa Specials).
Steam Working: Trains operate on Sundays and Bank Holidays from Easter until the end of October. There are also 'Santa Specials' on the three Sundays leading up to Christmas.
Prices: Adult £1.50
Child £1.00
Family Tickets £3.50

Detailed Directions by Car:
Travel by the A59 from Liverpool or Preston or by the A565 from Southport to the junction of the two roads at Tarleton. From here follow signs to Hesketh Bank. The Railway is signposted.

WEST SOMERSET RAILWAY

Address: The Railway Station, Minehead, Somerset TA24 5BG
Telephone Nº: (01643) 704996 (enquiries), (01643) 707650 (Talking timetable)
Year Formed: 1976
Location of Line: Bishops Lydeard (near Taunton) to Minehead

Length of Line: 19¾ miles
Nº of Steam Locos: 9
Nº of Other Locos: 13
Nº of Members: 3,500
Annual Membership Fee: £11.00
Approx Nº of Visitors P.A.: 145,000
Gauge: Standard

GENERAL INFORMATION

Nearest Railtrack Station: Taunton (4 miles)
Nearest Bus Station: Taunton (4½ miles) – Services 28 & 28A run to Bishops Lydeard
Car Parking: Free parking at Bishops Lydeard; Council car parking at Minehead
Coach Parking: As above
Souvenir Shop(s): Yes – at Minehead, Bishops Lydeard and Washford
Food & Drinks: Yes – At some stations. Buffet cars on steam trains

SPECIAL INFORMATION

Britain's longest Heritage railway runs through the Quantock Hills & along Bristol Channel Coast. Ten Stations with museums at Washford & Blue Anchor.

OPERATING INFORMATION

Opening Times: March to December. Daily from May to September. Open 9.30am to 5.30pm
Steam Working: All operatings days except Diesel Galas.
Prices: Adult £8.60
Child £4.30
Family £21.50 (2 adults + 2 children – up to 3 additional children travel for £1.00 each)

Detailed Directions by Car:
Exit the M5 at Taunton (Junction 25) and follow signs for A358 to Williton and then the A39 for Minehead. In Minehead, brown tourist signs give directions to the railway.

RAILWAY CIGARETTE & TRADE CARDS

We have a limited stock of cigarette and trade cards available, postage free, as follows : –

Issuer	Year	Set	Qty.	Price
JOHN PLAYER & SONS	1976	The Golden Age of Steam	24 lge.	£6.00
TADDY & CO.	1980	Railway Locomotives	26 std.	£5.00
HOBBYPRESS GUIDES	1984	Preserved Steam Railways 2nd	20 std.	£1.25
HOBBYPRESS GUIDES	1982	Victorian Steam Railway Miniprints	24 lge.	£7.50

SPECIAL OFFER – Buy all 4 of the above sets for just *£14.00*

Order from : –

MARKSMAN PUBLICATIONS
72 ST. PETERS AVENUE
CLEETHORPES
N.E. LINCOLNSHIRE
DN35 8HU

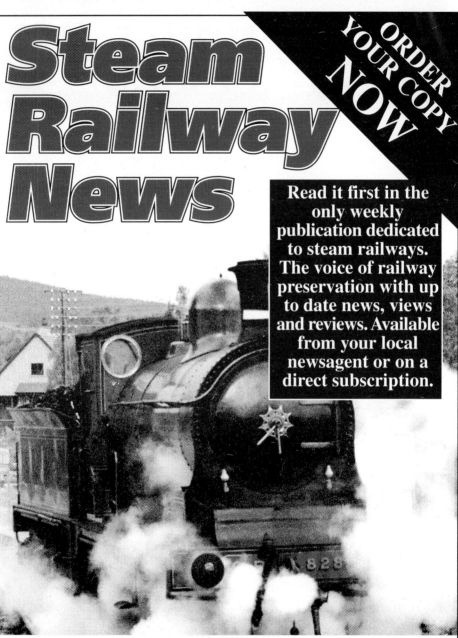